About th

Patrick Noonan is a Francisc
in Europe, the Middle East and the black townships of
South Africa since 1970 and was still there when his area
– known as the Vaal Triangle – exploded in anti-apartheid
rage in 1984. It was this uprising that signalled the
beginning of the end of apartheid and led to the release of
Nelson Mandela. He is presently ministering in Boksburg,
South Africa and also assists the Gauteng Council of
Churches in the area of post-apartheid reconciliation.
Besides articles for various books and magazines Noonan
has authored *They're Burning the Churches* (Jacana
2003) a best seller on crisis ministry and *Township God*
(Write-on Publishing 2017) on how he found God in non-
European cultures.

Noonan is also the recipient of the Mayor's Medal
for services to the communities in the Sedibeng district
municipalities, south of Johannesburg, South Africa.

ST FRANCIS UNCENSORED

BY

PATRICK NOONAN

Front cover photograph – Ancient door of the home of St Francis.
Photo Bente Wolf Assisi Mission, Assisi

Monument to parents of St Francis Pietro and Pica Bernardone by Roberto
Joppolo in front of Chiesa Nova, Assisi.

"Smell of the sheep" (Pope Francis) Pastors, religious and lay people will be comfortable reading this provocative tome which challenges many things you ever believed about those two spiritual trendsetters, Francis and Clare. You have been warned.

Ciaran O' Nuanain OFM, long-time pastor in war-torn El Salvador and presently coordinator of a project which researches the lives of the lay martyrs who were murdered during the civil war of the eighties.

In St Francis Uncensored, Patrick Noonan provokes thought on how to indigenise Francis today, how to make Francis at home in all cultures. His method is both dialogical and reflective while challenging the reader to action. To those who claim to be followers of St Francis, lay or religious, he throws a challenge. Be the Franciscans you claim to be. To leaders in Africa (and elsewhere) he argues that if the immense vision of Francis is accepted by ordinary people leadership will in turn be influenced to be more accountable and transparent to all citizens.

Richard Kakeeto, OFS, coordinator Justice and Peace Programmes, Centre for Social Justice and Ethics (CUEA) Programme Officer (pro bono) JPIC Franciscans Africa, Kenya.

I have never read a life of St Francis like this!

Dominic Hession OFM, well-known retreat director, formally deported by the apartheid government, pastor in many South African ghettos.

What a joy to once again read, reflect and meditate on Patrick Noonan's insights. He is original, authentic, and he has walked the talk for over fifty years on the peripheries. He continues to inspire. Read this book, share it with your family and friends and allow yourself to be transformed. Let your view of our Franciscan world be turned upside down.

Edward "Teddy" Lennon OFM, former embedded township pastor during the final uprisings against apartheid, presently serving in a Namibian parish while working with war veterans in the area of Justice, Peace and Healing of Memories.

Patrick Noonan's experience of living and working in the townships of an apartheid South Africa gives him a unique perspective on the life experience of St. Francis, who was counter cultural in relation to conflict, exercise of power, use of resources, love for the excluded and relationship with people of other faith traditions. This book, *St Francis, Uncensored*, renews our hope that a world of justice, peace and the integrity of creation is still possible, despite so many contradictory signs in today's world.

Gearóid Ó Conaire OFM – worked in El Salvador and then in Justice, Peace and Integrity of Creation animation for the Franciscans and a joint international commission of the leadership of men and women religious (USG/UISG).

St Francis has versatile appeal. To some he is the proto-hippie who renounced materialism and preached to the birds. To others he was the adamantly faithful son of the Church, or the reformer, or the eco-warrior, or the ascetic mystic, or the apostle to the poor, or the peacemaker. Or a broth of all or some of these ingredients.

For Patrick Noonan, St Francis is all of these, but more.

Significantly, Noonan shines a light on St Francis the peacemaker, noting that his unconventional initiative in mediating with the Muslim rulers at Crusader-besieged Damietta would have found very little favour in Christendom. Yet the Damietta initiative showed a new kind of peacemaking, through negotiation, respect and giving courageous witness in situations of war. This is indeed an important book.

Günther Simmermacher, editor The Southern Cross Catholic Newspaper Cape Town

When you open a book by Patrick Noonan you know you are going to be provoked. "St Francis Uncensored" is no exception. The author writes with a spontaneity and freshness that brings the real Francis of Assisi to the audience of today. Gone are the images of bird baths, and pious tales. Instead the author draws on his own experience of a lifetime spent among the poorest of the poor in Apartheid South Africa to establish fascinating links between the thirteenth century and our own time. His description of Francis as a "loose canon" making peace with the "Osama Bin Laden" of his day in the Middle East is a challenge to all of us as we face an ever-increasing sense of insecurity about peace in our world. "St Francis Uncensored" will open your eyes.

Hugh McKenna ofm President of the English Speaking Conference of Ministers Provincial

Over the centuries St Francis has become covered up with the sort of sentimental piety that obscures the real man and his associates, such as St Clare (called here "the indomitable pest of Popes"). Noonan wants to cut through all that, and also to explain a little about the outlook of the Pope.

The book compares the new movement St Francis started with the sort of activists we find today working among the poor of the world, and explores the image that St Francis has among Muslims after his pastoral visit to Egypt in 1219. The second part of the book dealing with this topic deserves to be widely read, but so to do the other parts. A 'revisionist' book, with the emphasis on the vision.

Peter Costello, The Irish Catholic

Dedication

To Mam, Secular Franciscan, who went home to the Lord in 2015 after a waiting period of 101 years.

To Richard "Bricks" Mokolo, fearless Catholic activist, apartheid torture survivor and international water warrior, who still speaks truth to power and gently reminds we religious people of our cutting-edge calling.

Acknowledgements

May I thank all who in different ways made this project possible: my Franciscan brothers and sisters, especially Liam McDermott who generously and patiently read and advised on the drafts as they appeared, Francis Cotter and Vumile Nogemane for their expert advice here and there, and historian Stephen O'Kane for moving things forward just at the right moment. Titans in the ministry of presence and accompaniment since the 1980s in different conflict areas of the world inspired me to press on when the way wasn't always clear: Ciaran O'Nuanain (El Salvador), Brendan Forde (Columbia), Lucas Bambezela, Dominic Hession (South Africa) Gearoid O'Conaire (El Salvador) and Teddy Lennon (South Africa and Namibia). Our constant sharing of pastoral ideas and spirituality from the frontiers is the backdrop to this volume. It is, therefore, a new world interpretation of Assisi.

I thank dear Biddy Greene of Cape Town for her meticulous, patient editing – and her always valuable suggestions. It was a time when Pope Francis was publishing his best sellers, *The Joy of the Gospel* and *Laudato Si* (encyclical on the Earth as our only home), which suddenly globalised in a new way St Francis's *Canticle of the Creatures*.

My publisher, Choice Publishing, has produced this handsome book. Thank you, Michelle Bradley and Deirdre Devine, for making the operation so pleasant and run so smoothly.

When writer Dolores Walshe (*Where the Trees*

Weep, Wolfhound Press 1992) appeared on the scene and looked over the proposed project the effects were seismic – in favour of producing a St. Francis blockbuster!

Behind the scenes a very willing back-up squad kept me fit, focused and forward looking: Marie Clerkin, Michael Noonan, Mairead Gormley, Jacinta Sequeira, Imelda O Luanaigh, Theresa Kelly and Paddy Lennon.

Table of Contents

An Age of Tribal Uprisings and "World" Wars: Timeline 1182–1228

1182	Francis Bernadone is born in Assisi while his father is away on business.
	Frederick Barbarossa is Holy Roman Emperor.
	War talk of another Crusade to the Holy Land.
	Banishment of Jews decreed in France.
1193	Clare Offreduccio is born in Assisi.
	Henry VI is Holy Roman Emperor, battling to conquer and consolidate the southern parts of Italy from where, it is thought, marauding Muslim mercenaries would later attack Clare's convent.
	Celestine III is Pope.
	Hildegard of Bingen is still alive, but Saladin has died.
1179	Agnes, Clare's sister, is born.
	Third Lateran Council.
1189	Uprising of citizens of Assisi against the German occupying forces in the fortress above the city.
	Third Crusade gets underway.
	Henry II of England invades France.
1202	Battle between Assisi and Perugia in which Francis is caught and imprisoned; Clare's family flee to Perugia as refugee nobles from Assisi. (Nobles from different towns customarily stayed together.)
1203	Late in the year Francis is released, probably for a ransom paid by his well-off merchant

(not noble) family. Meanwhile the Fourth Crusade is pillaging Constantinople.

1205–1210 Francis's conversion period. He makes a pilgrimage to Rome; his prayer life intensifies; encounter with leper; voice of the crucifix in San Damiano and subsequent repair of churches; first experience of poverty; he renounces his family's wealth; nursing lepers in Gubbio; first companions; gets his directions from the Gospel of Matthew (10: 7–20); writes a letter to the faithful; has his rule approved by Pope Innocent III.

1207 Elizabeth – later St Elizabeth, and a prominent secular Franciscan – is born of the royal family of Hungary.

1212 Eighteen-year-old Clare flees home to join the Franciscans.
Francis is shipwrecked on a mission to Syria.

1213 Francis's mission to Morocco also fails, due to his ill health.

1214 The Dominican Order is founded.

1215 Francis meets Dominic.
Magna Carta signed in England by King John.
Lateran IV abolishes trials by fire.

1216–1218 Francis organises the new Order; Chapters; meetings with the new Pope, Honorius III, who grants the Portiuncula Indulgence.

1219 The Franciscan Chapter (general gathering) sends friars to various European countries.
Francis leaves on his Damietta peace journey where he meets the Sultan on about

	22 September. Damietta is taken by John of Brienne, King of Jerusalem.
1220	Francis returns home.
1221	Crusaders abandon Damietta.
1223	Francis's Rule approved by Pope Honorius III.
	Francis resigns from leadership of Order. The amazing liturgy of the Greccio crib. (At this time the hill town of Mapungubwe in South Africa was a flourishing society of cattle farmers, miners, traders and artists).
1224	Francis receives the stigmata on Mount La Verna.
	The first Franciscan friars reach England and settle in Oxford and Cambridge.
1225	Francis has eye treatment at Fonte Colombo; composition of *The Canticle of the Creatures* at San Damiano.
1226	Death of Francis during the reign of King Louis IX of France.
1228	Canonisation of Francis.

Foreword

In Catholic bookshops there's a plethora of books on Pope Francis. After his election there was a new one almost every day. You might almost think the Pope was St Francis himself reincarnated. These books are written by European and American writers desperately trying to interpret the mind of non-European Pope Francis for their First World readership. Some are discovering that the Pope sees the world from a dynamic missionary standpoint; a position developed in the southern hemisphere, and lived by his role model St Francis of Assisi. Indeed, as *Time* (September 28, 2015) tells it "his life and outlook are the products of the developing world". Since I live in the global south, I bring something of that perspective to this book and will try to clarify what Pope Francis sees in the man known as the poor man of Assisi.

Of course it doesn't stop there.

To give you a hint of what's before us in this book: there are questions no First Worlder would dream of asking. Why is it that Islamists in Africa and the Middle East respect the brown Franciscan habit? (A friar just back from Kenya told me that in certain Islamic areas there he feels safe only when he's wearing the habit.) I knew that would surprise you. And how has the violence of Argentina in the 1970s influenced the thinking, and urgency of Pope Francis in his recent bestselling exhortation, *Evangelii Gaudium* (The Joy of the Gospel)? But let us not get ahead of ourselves.

An acclaimed Irish movie maker, while speaking to a group of eager movie students recently, said the following: "Who do you meet? Do you ever meet the poor in your area? Do you know who the local prostitutes are? Do you know who is suffering from terminal illness in your town? Do you ever meet the people in the old folk's home? Do you meet the powerful and the moneyed? Or the youth stranded between digital space, the ruins of religion and the drug zones? If you are not exposed to such a range of people, you will never come to know the depth of this society, and your film will have no force or truth." If serious movie makers show such passion for their work, if they are so focused on their market, their audience – the ordinary people of this world – then we Christians have something to learn from them.

Their singular and unselfish dedication to their craft must inspire us.

Christ expected all Christians to be teachers and heralds of a better world. Christ expected Christians to be in the business of enthusiastically marketing His life, death and Resurrection as a sign of hope, of peace and salvation for the people of all times – including our own time. St Francis, too, during his time in the thirteenth century, emerges from the mists of a European medieval landscape to become the most creative, daring and even outrageous saint that ever walked the hills and valleys of central Italy and beyond. Single-handedly, and with enormous zeal and purpose (all founders of religious congregations seem to be like this), Francis set out on an unstoppable journey that would significantly expose him to people and events from every level of feudal society: from popes to paupers, from kings to knaves, from princes to peasants, from soldiers to serfs.

This small book is a tentative exploration of his personality, a probe behind the domesticated image, a different window on his personal struggle for meaning. It is about how he discovered and managed what God was calling him to do and to be – then, and for us in the future.

I am exploring a Francis who lived in a pre-industrial era where life for the poor was short, cheap and brutally bloody. He lived in the time of action men like the mythical Robin Hood and his merry men. And, while I have little experience of verdant forests like good old Friar Tuck, I have lived like most missionaries in raw impoverished situations and so have some idea of the unpredictability and fragility of life. Perhaps I'm a secondary witness all the way from the peripheries so often mentioned by the present Pope, and lived by St Francis. This is the Francis I attempt to depict. The man from the margins, the outsider, the misfit.

I am writing about a Francis who grew up in a strongly Third World atmosphere, where culture was slow-moving, rural, and changing only slowly, if at all. It was however a world in transition, as Archbishop Slattery of South Africa notes: "The old world was changing. The population was rising, merchandising had begun. Roads were being constructed, towns were growing and great numbers of people were moving into towns as little industries began." In the same manner squatter communities mushroomed in the towns and cities of South Africa after apartheid.

Like ours, it was a world where the rich were getting richer and the poor poorer.

My Francis, while robustly loyal to the Church, clearly differed from the Pope in discerning the signs of the times. His loyal dissent led him to spend some quality time of another type in northern Africa, trying to bring peace where medieval civilisations – called East and West – were clashing on the bloody battlefields of Damietta. This will be covered in some detail in the later pages of the book.

The Francis in this book is not a Francis who has been created by serious First World scholars or by passionate animal lovers from the leafy suburbs of New York, Dublin, Berlin, London or Johannesburg. He is much more than that as we will see. This book is about a Francis immersed in wars, at a time when "honour" killings and family status were the name of the game. Where revenge, ISIS Middle Eastern style, was normal. In world history it was the golden era of head hunting! Archbishop Slattery continues:

> Italy and central Italy in the times of St Francis was a land totally in conflict. Village fought against village, city against city. There was no national government, no national police; it was an insecure country where people wreaked great cruelty on each other.

Don't even ask what crime and retribution was like. Suffice it to say that everyone was armed at all times except, according to Francis's later wish, his lay followers. Even in peacetime – and they barely knew what the word meant – family dungeons, yes, *family* dungeons, were commonplace to sort out upstart or erring offspring.

Our Francis comes to us out of these sometimes torrid family and civil relationships, relationships conditioned by ancient feuds, often-bitter rivalries, and intense tribal loyalties. The conflict areas of our present world show that things don't change much.

What do readers from the West know about the dynamics of tribal politics? Of the pre-industrial internecine quarrels of another age? How people lived in those turbulent and brutal times? There are parts of our world today where similar outlooks on life still shape the future of countries and regions.
The clan, the tribe, the family.

In the time of Francis, populations were not only growing but were coming together near cities – especially in the case of the migrating poor. Medieval squatter settlements were the result. Something similar is happening in the modern satellite townships of Africa and Asia today, as I have mentioned earlier. I have lived in African semi-urban, semi-squatter-camp situations for nearly forty years. When people live right on top of one another, a new and different set of dynamics governs their day-to-day lives. They learn new ways of behaviour, of living, of hoping, of coping with the proximity of neighbours, of relating to others, of avoiding quarrels and disputes, indeed of surviving. Social cohesion is worked out through trial and error – and not always peacefully. But there is more to it than that. It must not be assumed that we, the affluent, know how the poor live, today or yesterday or yesteryear. When people live in informal settlements – today or in Francis's time – the inside story is endless.

Imagine you are in Assisi in the time of Francis or Clare. Let us for a moment leave the piazza and make our way through the old town. Perhaps we'll meet some people for a chat. There is so much to learn about the human spirit of people living in close quarters on narrow lanes. It's obvious that everyone knows where everyone else is living; what lane, which dark side passageway, through what short cut, or near which important person's house. They say you can never get lost here. But I don't know; the labyrinth of narrow twisting streets and alleyways don't have names as we know them today. I'm weary I won't fit in here, I'm thinking. It's claustrophobic.

Coraggio, says my friendly guide and off we go into the bowels of the medieval town of Assisi. There are so many people coming and going in these sunless passageways each to their own small space chatting, laughing and shouldering their way past us. Oops, was that Francis Bernardone who just passed us now as we were talking? Did you see him? Possibly coming from a meeting with the priests at San Rufino church. A troubled man, he's looking, these days. Perhaps depressed. The church was in a mess in those times. Some priests could hardly pronounce the Latin at Mass, others were supporting children on the side. And as for the corruption and money scandals … But years later, more attuned to the merciful mind of God, less judgemental and less indignant, Francis would come to understand the flawed face of the Body of Christ, the Church. The struggles, sins and weaknesses of its priests, while by no means excusable, would begin to evoke his compassion and forgiveness.

The noisy chatter on the streets of Assisi is ceaseless and endless. It's like one giant, spread-out, busy kitchen where everyone is gossiping at the same time about local political and family affairs. The intimate family things these people talk about in public! Nobody says, "Keep your voice down" or "What will the neighbours think?" It doesn't apply here. These people don't think that way. They don't hide, perhaps can't hide, things. It's all one big extended family, like you have in Africa and Asia and some European countries. Well, nearly like that. People live differently because of their historic circumstances. When a new baby is born it's an occasion of community rejoicing. The same for weddings, or when you are having visitors. It's everyone's business to rejoice and welcome the stranger. Sharing and fellowship are key factors in community living here in Assisi. The correcting of younger children is the responsibility of the community, in the sense, unlike today, that any adult could reprimand anyone's naughty child, and indeed are expected to do that.

All these social factors influenced Francis's later life with the poor.

Security. If you had the money and lived in upper suburban Assisi you could have your own militia to protect the family. Otherwise policing wasn't too sophisticated. Probably there was vigilantism where the community dealt with bullies and criminals in a predictable way guided by the needs of the immediate situation.

The Francis of this book emerges from this milieu. If you have seen pictures of the wonderfully excavated Capharnaum, the city of Jesus, you will note that Christ lived for some years in similar neighbourhoods on the shores of the Sea of Galilee. G. K. Chesterton believed that Christianity hadn't been sufficiently tried; this book humbly suggests that the historic St Francis – the real man – hasn't yet been sufficiently analysed and explored. The book has been written by an embedded missionary who has seen and lived other realities, who has discovered the God of poor cultures and been confronted by other human motivations, situations, illuminations, revelations, values and explanations of things often hidden from Western experience, or even the trained academic eye. I found Francis in these diverse circumstances. Francis has often been presented to us from the upper reaches of stained-glass windows in ornate churches, from the fabulous paintings of a tortured soul seeking God in the solitude of a cave, or on Mount La Verna in ecstasy receiving the stigmata before the seraph from Heaven. Behind all this was the struggling human being, trying to make sense of astonishing things happening in his life. In this book I attempt to capture some of the historical context of that humanity from which his sainthood developed.

Breaking News in Assisi

Photo: Russel Murray, ofm, NY

Today in downtown Assisi the devastated parents of Francis Bernadone held a media briefing to try to explain the disappearance of their beloved son, Francis. "He was such a cheerful person, a model son with a successful career in front of him, loved by all and so popular with his peers," his weeping mother sobbed. "We can't understand what got into him at all."

The distraught mother, Pica, was holding the severed chains once used by the family to restrain their son during a family feud. Her husband, the well-known international textile dealer Pietro Bernadone, showed the media some of the clothes his son was wearing before he ran away. Business colleagues present at the gathering suggested that he might have been sucked into a recent breakaway religion some of whose members were known to be in Assisi. Privately this struck a chord with the parents because a priest, a family friend, had called on the Bernadone home to tell the family that Francis himself was attracting followers not only inside the city but outside too.

The police are following a number of leads and appealed to Assisians to remain calm and report any unusual religious gatherings in their area of town or among the peasants in the lowlands outside.

Holding hands, the Bernadones asked for privacy at this time while they come to terms with this unhappy family misfortune.

26 April, 1218. From our correspondent, Assisi Times

PART 1

THE LOVE LIFE OF FRANCIS AND CLARE

No one has better achieved the unity and integrity of all elements than did Saint Francis in the realm of the religious, the erotic, social relations, art and knowledge – *Max Scheler* (1874–1928)

I ask dear Jesus to draw us ever more into the recesses of his heart, and make us one in his love, and use us as an instrument of his healing love for others.
– *St Francis's blessing of St Clare and her sisters* (from *The Legend of Perugia* c. 1311)

Chapter 1

The Facts

Don't call me a saint; I could still make children – *Attributed to St Francis after he received the stigmata*

The heart has reasons that reason does not understand – *Jacques Benigne Bossuel*

The background facts as we know them about the lifelong friendship of Francis and Clare are the following:

They were born at the same time in history. They were born in the same town and baptised in the same cathedral in upmarket Assisi. Their families were known to each other but were on different, very entrenched, political sides in the bloody conflict between Perugia and Assisi.

Both intentionally renounced the comfortable upper-class status of their families. Both, against the wishes of their families, espoused the cause of poorness. Primed for fashionable society weddings, they both choose not to get married, and in the process broke off relationships with sweethearts and suitors their parents were planning for them.

Francis and Clare, according to Franciscan historian Vumile Nogemane, initially lived in Benedictine monasteries. I'm sure their bishop hoped they would stay there. But the two youngsters had other plans.

Later, Clare and Francis, with inspired zeal, went on to establish new forms of religious life in the Church. They founded three new orders, including an Order for the laity not based on the established monastic system of the time. During this process they often consulted one another about the practicalities of the rules and constitutions of, for that time, their strange new orders.

Both pressurised Church authorities for many years to achieve their very single-minded aims. Both insisted on personal contact with the Pope to approve their radical ideas and actions.

This worried the bishops, especially the cardinals of the Church.
Unlike breakaway discontents of the time they stayed within the fold even when it looked ugly and degenerate.

Finally, both were nourished by a similar and singular spirituality which they had gradually discovered and embraced through humble submission to the promptings of God.

These are the facts. God was behind these facts. He made them happen. They were the fruits of his love; nothing was an accident. God, through this unlikely pair, was renewing his dysfunctional church. He raised up Francis and Clare to address the world, to propose an alternative way of life, to return to the basics of Christianity. In this divine plan God expected them to work out the minor details of how their relationship would blossom and sustain itself. They were to become spiritually closer to one another – even closer than most married people deeply in love. If this had been a marriage it would have been the proverbial "marriage made in Heaven". Each fact, every event, drew them closer together. It was inevitable; it was irresistible. Unbreakable forces were binding them together, bonding their intimacy and cementing their relationship.

It went very deep indeed. Deeper than we can imagine.

According to Poor Clare, Sister Bernadette Coughlan, (Ennis Convent, Ireland) Francis and Clare shared a single world view and calling even before they had followers. "It was a spiritual bond born through the enlightenment of the Holy Spirit, and later sealed when Clare, together with her sisters, promised obedience to Francis". Moreover, Francis, as we have mentioned elsewhere, often came to Clare for help and advice during times of frustration and difficulties. And these were many. It is no surprise then as Sister Bernadette says that "the very different ways in which Francis and Clare lived the same call, but so equal in radicalism and passion, have fascinated men and women from every social, racial and cultural background over the past eight hundred years".

In Assisi, after they both sensationally renounced their families – no gentle leave-taking with tissues and tears – they became items at the festivals; the stuff of tabloids today. "Did you hear the latest about the Bernadone boy and that Offreduccio girl?" the upper crust wives chattered knowingly, "they're involved" they gushed, in gales of laughter. Since Francis and Clare came from such well-known, distinguished families you can imagine the impact on the town. The city gossip mill was in overdrive. The rumour machine was unstoppable; the whispers unquenchable. "But would you let your daughter marry one of them?" hissed someone darkly – because there was even talk that they had eloped – and both from two distinct and separate social classes in the town, like a black person and a white person breaking the colour bar and eloping during apartheid South Africa. It was a cause for worry among fundamentalists, among the class-conscious purists. "Had their parents no control over them?" somebody spat with venom. This was a society proud of its class and social distinctions. There was a hierarchy of status, with different levels of dignity running through society, and these rules of life were strictly adhered to. Letting the side down just wasn't tolerated.

Let us ponder the social backgrounds of Francis and Clare, the political allegiances of their families. These were not peaceful times. Skirmishes, wars, battles and faction fighting were almost daily facts. Like the Wild West as we said earlier: you walked around armed or you were stupid. Bloody drunken brawls and honour duels were commonplace. Enter Francis, and Clare, twelve years his junior. Francis was at one time imprisoned · during the violent class struggle with the neighbouring

Perugians. During this battle, Clare and her well-off *noble* family had to flee Assisi and take refuge in Perugia. Francis's class, the *business people*, had chased them out. So there was a power struggle between the wealthy business elite on the one side and the nobles on the other. Yes, they went to war over things like that.

But they did too, over Communism and Nazism, in the twentieth century.

"So Francis's and Clare's families were very definitely on different sides of the bitter conflict", according to Franciscan scholar Francis Cotter. This baggage of struggle, strife, violence and rigid class distinctions was probably initially unquestioned – ingrained and in their very make-up. Both came from the upper classes where "breeding, stock and blood" emphasised their innate superiority over the wild and uncouth lower classes. These qualities were the early dawnings of racial discrimination based on biology and culture. By the 16th century the word *race* began to refer to family, lineage and breed. They grew up in a literally divided landscape where, as Irish poet Seamus Heaney put it: "the lines of sectarian antagonism and affiliation followed the boundaries of the land".

Francis and Clare carried unconscious genteel upper-class mannerisms of their affluent upbringing into their new religious life. We who have taken vows and live in community under the same roof know that you don't unbundle, you don't unpack your received personality DNA all that quickly, even when you join religious life. Although, as we draw closer to Christ – like Peter discovering that he was just a sinful fisherman – we may lose or shed our useless differences and the sharp corners that we came with. Francis and Clare both probably had many stories to tell from life on opposite sides of the political spectrum. They both emerged from a stratified society that revered status and class rather than patriotism and loyalty to hometown. And I'm sure that was an influence on their future decisions to disconnect, to make a clean break with the past.

Francis was now a political detainee in a dark stinking Perugian dungeon, while Clare and her family, newly arrived from Assisi, were up town living in luxury and doing what nobles did that time: enjoying equestrian tournaments, archery contests and matchmaking their (mostly compliant) sons and daughters. In fact our Francis was lucky he hadn't been executed in a tank of boiling water after his capture by the others. After his release, probably negotiated by his family, Francis and Clare began to make waves across the busy town. Who could have guessed what was in the air, who was seeing whom, and where it was all going to lead to? Of course, close friends of both families confirmed the rumours. Still, it took a lot of time for most people to get a handle on the real facts. To make a long story shorter: Assisi witnessed two very messy and public family blow-ups, perhaps the most well-documented in Christian history. The good names and reputations of the Bernadone and Offreduccio families, possibly the most prominent families in the city, were brought into disrepute and disgrace. The unthinkable had happened. Thanks to their shameless offspring, recriminations abounded between the two families when it became clear that Francis was the leader (even though Clare was a very willing follower). And what made it worse, some allowed, was that the

Church itself was involved – pulling the strings in the background. It was like a medieval soap opera. The pull and thrust of a feudal *Days of Our Lives*, or perhaps more like *Downton Abbey*.

Chapter 2

The Legends

Will Francis get his Clare? Will their mothers, Pica and Ortolana, speak to each other after Mass on Sunday? Will they even look at one another? – *Perugia Post (26 June 1216)*
What did the bishop whisper so publicly to Clare during Mass on Palm Sunday morning? – *Assisi Times (2 July 1216)*
Why is it so shocking to have no sex life? – *Sunday Times headline (18 August 2013)*

Now let us see how Clare and Francis in fact responded to the challenge. How they pursued their dreams in the context of this amazing scenario. God in his wisdom allowed them the space and freedom to connect and interact all through their lives. It wasn't always easy either. Perhaps it was a little like the following.

For those who need to know (and voyeuristic labelling is so trendy today), Francis was very definitely heterosexual. He had at least two lady friends. Yes, he had at least two women friends who loved him dearly and cared for him tenderly in every way possible. They were ready to comfort and affirm him in whatever way they could. He knew this and, as in most love affairs, he responded as appropriately as possible; as appropriately as he could at any given moment, in the context of his short, eventful life. Capuchin friar Fr Raniero Cantalamessa cautiously goes into more detail: "Francis, like any other man, even if he is a saint, may well have experienced the attraction of women and the call of sex." And why not? It's not as if Francis was a monk on Mount Athos in Greece where females – half of the human race – are banned. He enjoyed the company of people but he wasn't a compulsive socialiser. Ask the parents. He didn't hide away from the adoring maidens who undoubtedly pursued him in his early life. After all he had been a playboy and soldier, and later wandered the known world as a peacemaking mendicant, with a religious companion for company and security (two by two as enjoined in the Gospel). And he knew all about temptations too. Why do we doubt this just because he turned out to be a saint? If Jesus encountered them, why not Francis? In his early life he would have had the same feeling as Oscar Wilde, who famously admitted to a fawning, delighted society audience, "I can resist everything except temptation."

But a time came when Francis had to forgo the implications of this frivolous remark. It did not fit in comfortably with his changing way of life. A time came when he felt called to resist the seductive lures of life in the fast lane, lures in general such as consumerism, materialism, hedonism, violence and a dash of lust here and there. Indeed a time was to come when he would take extraordinary measures to survive serious sexual temptation. Fr Raniero again: "The sources tell us that in order to overcome a temptation of this kind the saint once rolled (naked) in the snow in the depths of winter". The powerful sexual fantasies present needed drastic action, and Francis responded drastically. Not the way agony aunts would recommend nowadays! Another time at Greccio (he must have told someone next morning) he had sexual cravings throughout the night until he realised he was using a feathered pillow. He threw it away and the temptation ceased. (Note: This should not be taken as a universal antidote for all who are battling night-long temptations!). Could you imagine people doing that nowadays? Francis, with his vividly inventive mind, did it his way, long before Frank Sinatra got the idea. These are legends that have come down to us. They help us to understand St Francis's earthly journey and to appreciate the richness of his character.

Chapter 3

Was St Francis an Exhibitionist?

(Francis) a savage madman who ran around naked – *Voltaire (1694–1778)*

Yes, Francis threw himself naked into the snow as we have just said. This raises an interesting question. If I remember correctly Francis, according to the records, went naked in public on at least three occasions: when outside the bishop's palace he declared that God was his only father; as above, jumping into the snow to control his sensual craving of lust; and finally when he begged on his death pallet to meet the Crucified Lord, stripped of all earthly possessions.

His relationship with God certainly didn't deter him from stripping in front of people. Perhaps public nudity wasn't illegal in those times. Maybe it was more common in medieval times. When on a visit to Assisi in 2015 here's what Pope Francis said about his namesake St Francis who stripped one morning on a street in Assisi:

> Francis stripped himself of everything, and stood naked before his father, the bishop, the people of Assisi and indeed God. It was a prophetic gesture, and it was also an act of prayer, an act of love and of entrustment to the Father who is in Heaven. With that

gesture, Francis made his choice, the choice to be poor ... Francis stripped himself of everything of his worldly life and of himself to follow his Lord, Jesus, to be like him. Bishop Guido understood that gesture and rose immediately, embracing Francis and covering him with his cloak, and was always his aid and protector.

Yes, Francis loved the dramatic twist, the symbolic action – even if bordering on scandal – that drove his passion for union with God. Nowadays the only people who strip to make a point are streakers at major sports events. We have all seen TV pictures of anxious London bobbies chasing naked males (and sometimes females too) across sports fields or tennis courts, to the delight of cheering crowds. And if we're tempted to call them exhibitionists, then Francis was an exhibitionist too – an exhibitionist who became a saint.

I wonder was it his culture, or the times or his temperament, that drove him to these rather ostentatious flourishes of nakedness when he was upset? But maybe it was acceptable in his time. Maybe the naked body was viewed differently in those times. Isn't it the human body that inspired the genius of Italian art down through the centuries? It is carved in stone and marble in every piazza you care to visit in Italy. So maybe there was less shame attached to it then, less guilt or scrupulosity, so to say. One wonders, was he comfortable with his body? Comfortable enough, in a sense, to objectify it and try to press it into submission by beating it – as was customary. And he insisted that his followers take an uncompromising attitude to unlawful demands stalking their own bodies. A young aspiring Franciscan in a quiet moment once asked an older friar:

"Father, when do sexual temptations stop?"
"About a half hour after your death, laddie", came the wise reply.

Chapter 4

Francis and the Clerical Scandals. What's New?

What a man is in the sight of God, so much
he is and no more – *St Francis of Assisi*

If I had the use of my body I would throw it
out of the window – *Samuel Beckett, 1906 –
1989*

In some circumstances involving sexuality, or its misuse,
Francis was more spiritually enlightened than many of us
nowadays. He had to know that our bodies teach us
about the love of God and had been given to us by a
loving God. He must have known that only with our
bodies could we give, receive, provide, sacrifice and offer
love to God and one another. Never mind that we need it
for the World Series, the Olympic Games, the
Premiership, gambling and even *body*building itself.

But did he know it well enough to live by it
himself? Probably not, because later in life Francis
acknowledged that he had been a bit too harsh on
Brother Body or Brother Ass as he liked to call it. Oops,
so he had a sense of humour in all this! Ass. Today only
lower class Americans employ this term when referring to
posteriors. But perhaps Francis had a jackass in mind.
Who knows the mind of a saint? Acta Sanctae Sedis (ASS,
an international Vatican news letter) had not begun
publication in the twelfth century! While we're on

humour: When Brother Leo was having too many "visions" of Jesus Francis told him it was the devil in disguise. He advised Leo, with a twinkle in his eye to tell his "Jesus" next time that he was about to shit into his mouth.

Francis was, however, less judgemental than we are today. He could evaluate a situation and not take umbrage. Where we might be indignant, he was calm and understanding. Where we might be judgemental, Francis responded with compassion. Like the time when there was a priest in a certain town living openly with his comely girlfriend, to the anger and scorn of the parishioners. A great scandal, it was felt by all – nudge, nudge ... and it had been going on for some time. Enter Francis one fine morning. After Mass he goes to meet the embarrassed cleric, and promptly kisses his hands, because, he said, they are the hands that hold up the Eucharist.

When this kind of scandal happens today, for many it is a signal to leave the Church, the Body of Christ, and to seek the same Christ in other very human folds. But Francis didn't allow disloyalty, degenerate priests or corrupt bishops to separate him from the love of God or that of the church. That's the profound maturity found only in those living truly close to God and in a personal relationship with Jesus. The fact that these erring priests physically handled the Eucharist was enough for Francis. A merciful stance 800 years before Pope Francis proclaimed the Year of Mercy!

There is a further point of history to be noted here. It helps us to understand our present times. People have been leaving the church since the time of Christ. "Will you also go away?" our Saviour once remarked to the disciples. Fast forward to the thirteenth century of Francis. The decadence in the church that time sent many scurrying to discontented groups like the Albigensians and other sincere but heretical sects and cults. Or none at all. Personally I would have a problem deciding to leave a community, even a wounded community, claimed by Christ as his own. He is after all the centre of the universal Christian community. "Go repair my house (church)" Christ said to Francis that morning in San Damiano. He didn't say "Go leave my house"

And furthermore, he called the church *my* house. *My* house.

Francis's intentional celibacy was no different from the celibacy or partial celibacy enjoyed by millions in every walk of life down through the ages, for all sorts of reasons: ritual perhaps, or cultural, or career decisions, or from a strong desire to be single and independent, or for health reasons, perhaps, or gender conditions. However in his later life, as a celibate by choice and conviction, Francis nurtured the presence of God in a way that left little room for anything else. He could not tell when or at what moment the experiences of his heart edged beyond the frontiers of everyday life. But he silently noticed that his friends were not always on his wavelength, were not always understanding where he was coming from, and what was happening inside him.

It's so easy to talk in hindsight. Francis came to take very seriously Matthew 8:20: "I will be with you always", and John 1:14, where God tells us about "making his home among us". His intimacy with the Lord became a special way of loving, another way, a new way, a different way. This interior journey took a long time to mature. It doesn't follow, however, that Francis was immune to primitive yearnings, to the overwhelming emotional power of sexual attraction – the Godly eros and agape of human love – that mysterious and intense experience Pope Benedict addresses in his first encyclical letter, *Deus Caritas Est*. He wasn't, believe me.

So Francis experienced in his life an overpowering sexual energy, the "divine madness" which was to teach him so much about himself and the steps he had to take to channel positively the emotional side of his divine calling. Perhaps this "madness" helped him understand that the restless, erotic desires we feel – in both our bodies and our spirits – reveals the cry of our hearts for a loving God who ultimately satisfies every need.

Chapter 5

Francis Loved Jacoba's Gifts

*It is in loving that we are loved – attributed
to St Francis*
Now Jesus loved Martha ... – John 11:5

In the crypt where St Francis is buried in Assisi, there
also lie the mortal remains of "Brother" Jacoba. An old
colleague of St Francis. But who was "Brother" Jacoba?
you may ask. Jacoba was, in fact, a woman. (No, this is
not a Pope Joan scenario!) A dear friend of Francis. And
there she is buried next to the saint himself. Why did his
early followers allow this to happen, we might ask again?
But perhaps they didn't ask that question. Perhaps they
didn't need to. It was not an issue. They knew of her
kindnesses and knew it was a wholesome and fruitful
friendship. In order to protect their relationship, Francis
did not allow emotional intimacy to get the upper hand.
Rather he tried to treat Jacoba with the tender, caring
love that he wished would bind his brotherhood. He
demythologised her feminine mystique. It happens in the
workplace even today. He made her a brother. An
honorary brother. A neat way, even if sexist in today's
language, for handling a healthy, open relationship that
could be easily misconstrued.

The Catholic Culture website, as quoted by
Conventual friar Phil Kelly, says of her: "Jacoba, a very
devout woman and noted for her great generosity, often

gave lodging to the Poverello when he came to Rome. So impressed was he with the energy and the capability of his friend that he called her 'Br Jacoba'". The Lady Jacoba di Settesoli not only supported Francis's friars financially, she also saw to it that Francis kept in good shape. She gave him his favourite food, a sweetmeat called frangipane, a concoction of almonds and sugar, for which the saint expressed perhaps the only compliment on cooking in his life. This same Lady Jacoba came all the way from Rome when she heard Francis was dying, and brought candles for his bier, a new habit she had woven for him, incense, a pillow and, yes, some frangipane. But there is more to this than meets the eye. Mostly we've been given the male version of Francis's death perhaps for reasons of propriety, or some decision by the first friars. What would you expect a loving mother or friend to do at the bed of a dying daughter, son, husband, sister or brother?

Darleen Pryds, professor of history and spirituality at the Franciscan School of Theology (Oceanside, CA) attempts to restore some balance to the situation. She speaks of the femininity of this Jacoba, an early friend of the Order. She says of her:

> She likely held his hand or stroked his arm to offer him comfort. She may have cradled his head and offered him drops of water to ease his parched mouth and lips. And no doubt she prayed. Some of her prayers may have been silent; others she may have sung or spoken out loud. (*Today this deep felt spontaneous type of prayer and faith is mostly lost in the Western Church – author*)

She likely also attended to the friars who were anxiously witnessing the passing of their founder. To alleviate their stress, Jacoba may have gently embraced them or simply put her arm around them, comforting them in their uneasiness. Together they probably broke these moments of concern and hours of boredom by sharing favourite stories of Francis in order to pass the time as he lay dying." (*The Cord, Vol. 65, June 2015*)

Clearly this was a very human, warm relationship, sexual and spiritual in nature, but not genital. Today he would be called a sacrament to her.

The attraction of sex will always be there. It's built into our amazing bodily and mental machinery made in the image and likeness of God, and it influences our behaviour in friendships and in society. That's enough for me. Certainly it was enough for Francis. We are made to make love. We are supposed to find one another attractive. That's why some of us are beautiful, handsome, adorable, sexy, and charming. We are made to keep the erotic tension alive. The human race needs it, depends on it. Hollywood movies endlessly serve this purpose through the love interest that sustains and sells almost all movies. It's the most sustainable thing the movie moguls have. Sex always sells. Sex is mind-boggling, mind-bending and mind-blowing. And God made it that way. So let's celebrate it; let's celebrate the way God does things. Let's celebrate the God of sex. Of course, like with many other things, there's the downside, the exploitative, dark, seamier side to it which fuels the sex industry, and underlies human trafficking, prostitution, pornography and marital cheating.

With Lady Jacoba and Lady Clare two different relationships crossed the path of St Francis. I suspect Lady Jacoba was maybe even a mother figure to him, while Clare was a more emotional significance, and later a more spiritual figurehead and mentor. Initially perhaps Clare saw Francis as a social rebel, a local hero, a role model – and later a spiritual guide. They had the same vision but learned to keep an emotional distance, to maintain the integrity of their relationship. Both were simultaneously and creatively exploring new ground in religious life. This must have kept the local church authorities on their toes, to say nothing of the other traditional religious orders and congregations already in Assisi and environs. The founding of two new orders in the same town at the same time would make any bishop worried. And wary. And having the Pope involved in both cases was cause for great concern in clerical circles. Francis and Clare were on to something new in the life of the Church. And Francis was the ringleader. A born leader, with political talent, natural charm and a gift of persuasion.

The two saints were into a new project that required close consultation on a whole range of human and divine situations found in religious life. Rules, regulations, statutes and constitutions, prayer life, daily schedules, administration. She was founding the Poor Clares on Francis's inspiration and needed his constant advice on the day-to-day running of a new convent, a new Order, and a completely new form of religious life. A relationship of complementarity had to develop naturally between Francis and Clare. It wasn't all smooth and lovey-dovey. If only you could have heard the gossip in the surrounding monasteries, convents, presbyteries, and indeed city hall itself, when news began to break that Francis and Clare were starting some new movement against the wishes of their distinguished and now shaken families. Both, in gazing on the Lord together, their divine sweetheart, were making history: church history and human history. "Being in love does not mean looking at each other, but looking together in the same direction", wrote Antoine de Saint-Exupery, some seven hundred years later. They would have agreed.

Founding, if reluctantly, two new religious orders at the same time and in the same place was nothing less than awesome. It had also never been done before. Just think about it – how it would stir up things if it happened today. The church authorities were probably worried about Francis and Clare's misplaced enthusiasm for reform and change. As every decent bishop knows, reformers and prophets (though Francis and Clare never thought of themselves as reformers or prophets) are something else, not easy to handle, women or men. They can be very determined people, even stubborn, when a bishop doesn't seem to understand them. Bishops know these things: they will tell you. Now here we have two youngsters from the same town, determined to rock the boat, by implication to question the way things had always been done, and, if they don't get satisfaction, to go over the bishop's head, all the way to Rome. The Pope of Rome!

Actually Bishop Guido of Assisi, to be fair to him, did his best to accommodate them. He tried to understand. He tried to distinguish between the real thing and young intense religious fanatics who regularly came to the palace gates wanting Episcopal authorisation to save the world from perdition. These two, Francis and Clare, he thought, were different. There was something about them ... The bishop's secretary had pointed out to the bishop that they were not being strident or boisterous or impossible in their waywardness. They were not attacking the bishops or cardinals or the Pope or the Church. They were not given to angry outbursts or indiscretions. It seemed that they wanted to work from within the Church, even if they were more than non-conformist. The bishop's palace in Assisi was accommodating and took a benign position towards them. The cardinals in Rome, however, were a different kettle of fish. They were sceptical and doubtful. They felt this whole business of new orders and congregations was, shall we say, a bit messy – unpredictable and uncontrollable. Couldn't the Bernadone boy and Lady Ortolana's girl just join the Benedictines and be done with it, they muttered. It also mystified the princes of the Church no end that, although born into well-off families, the pair were busy searching for what is called today "a preferential option for the poor", being poor and being among the poor. How upsetting, how dangerous, indeed. They are so different. This was not done in polite circles. It was unheard of in Upper Assisi! The clergy discussed it among themselves. Episcopal opinion was divided. This Francis Bernadone from Assisi was the instigator. Perhaps it was actually a passing flirtation, or even a love affair, under the guise of religion, chimed in the Bishop of Capranica who happened to be visiting one day. He suggested asking Rome for an opinion.

If this were happening today someone would have called the police to rescue these young ones from the claws of this new poverty cult that was brainwashing them, and probably others too. You know these secretive cults with their spellbinding, charismatic, long-haired messiah leaders. And forbidding walled residences, to wit. This was the context of their relationship. This was what brought Francis and Clare together. A relationship of two people brought together, passionately involved with the same things, with a purpose that became ever more divine. And these divine matters seemed to take over their lives, their very existence – even to the point of diminishing or regulating the powerful role of sexuality in their relationship. Indeed, Francis was quite sensitive about the integrity of his relationship with Clare. Perhaps too sensitive. It is recorded that he became over-reserved in his interaction with Clare to the point where he was affectionately chided by his Franciscan brothers for being too harsh with her. Fr Raniero takes up the story again: "Only at the end of his life do we see this rigour in the relationship soften, and Francis visits his 'Little Plant' more and more frequently in search of comfort and confirmation". So Clare became a sort of mentor and affirmer to Francis in the later stages of his life.

And so it came to pass, our two young lovers didn't walk into an Italian sunset or richly blossoming vineyard, tenderly holding hands, gazing adoringly into each other's moist eyes, tongues salivating, lips parting in readiness. This is the part the media, the paparazzi won't like. The part that makes them wonder. The part they can barely relate to. The part they'll have to ring the editor for instructions about. A mystery landscape. Romantic love is not the winner in this case. There are no furtive meetings, no tender touches or sporadic tiffs as they get to know each other. It wasn't as if his arresting good looks captivated her; Francis was no Richard Gere or George Clooney. It's not a natural situation, and it doesn't have a predictable outcome. It's not the ending that we thought we wanted, even if it's a divinely ordained ending. The Assisi tabloids were devastated.

The fact of the matter was that the love of Clare and Francis was redirected, subsumed, and focused forward on the object of their intense desire, the Eucharist, the Lord, and the Crucified One. God is the link in the relationship that transforms them beyond recognition, beyond anything they could ever have dreamed of. Jesus had already pride of place in their throbbing hearts. And their commitment to Jesus as Lord was ongoing, and deepening. It guarded and protected their tender relationship. They in turn, in living their parallel lives, enriched the relationship with their own masculine and feminine qualities, sensitivities, intuitions, gifts and discernments.

It's worth remembering too that Francis didn't ask God to be the founder of an Order. Neither did Clare. They didn't ask to be born a few doors away from one another in affluent Assisi. They didn't ask God for the same dream, the same vision, the same outlook, the same motivation, the same inspiration. God gave them their vocations. He did the calling. They did the answering. He did the giving. They did the receiving – including almost the same family ruptures. It was God's gift. Made and managed in Heaven. God made it happen and led them to manage the consequences, come what might.

These were lives to remember, to inspire and to follow.

What a pair! Or with Lady Jacoba, what a trio!

Chapter 6

Clare the Indomitable Pest of Popes

You know, I believe that the Kingdom of Heaven is promised and given by the Lord only to the poor (cf. Matthew 5:3), for she who loves temporal things loses the fruit of love. Such a person cannot serve God and money, for either the one is loved and the other hated, or the one is served or the other is despised (cf. Matthew 6:24) – *St Clare in a letter to her sister, St Agnes of Assisi*

Her family didn't know what to do about Clare. How difficult she had become. They were disturbed and distressed. They were clearly suffering from post-traumatic stress syndrome. The talk of the town. As a rule pretty girls didn't leave the safety of their homes on moonless nights, and disguised, slip down through dark narrow streets of Assisi and then descend a mountainside for the next two hours in the hope of finding Francis and his merry men. Not done, period. Her mother, quite a religious woman who had made three pilgrimages to the Holy Land, tried to understand the will of God in the situation.

Clare's departure, or rather her escape – because that's what it was – had led to a huge family blow-up. "It is hard enough for us today to imagine how shocking this must have been – a young beautiful girl of eighteen going off on her own with a band of ragamuffin friars" (*P.4 Calm the Soul, The Poor Clares, Galway*) I have known girls in Africa who have abandoned kith and kin in order to follow their religious dreams. The bishop of Assisi, when he heard of her departure, for that's what he called it, was not amazed. He knew the family would be coming soon for explanations. Meanwhile, they actually sent armed security guards to capture and bring her back home. The girl didn't know what to think with the suddenness of it all. She didn't know they would react this way. She knew everyone by name who had come for her. They had been her minders, her protectors. Now her family servants had become her enemies. She knew the family name was at stake. It seriously pained her to bring her extended family into disrepute. Sudden doubts invaded her mind. It was nightmare beyond anything she had ever encountered. She felt a whisper of terror run through her as the possibility of violence loomed. All her inner warning-systems were going off at once. A physical tug of war ensued at the altar in the small church, until Clare pulled her veil aside to show them her tonsured head. What a dramatic moment of reckoning, of truth. The supercharged silence following this revelation stunned the family militia. They drew back in horror, in disbelief. It was then they realised the battle was lost. She had gone too far to the other side. She was now out of reach.

It was bizarre. The family gave up trying to stop her from following her desires. They had wanted her to follow *their* dreams for her, as was the custom – and she was having none of it. As far as they were concerned, it was all about family honour and noble status in society. They had a reputation to keep and Clare's inexplicable behaviour had caught everyone by surprise. Some blamed Francis for it. They spoke to his parents about it, but they were in a quandary themselves about Francis – their own boy.

Meanwhile, their rumoured affair was the talk of the town. The young lovers had vanished, so the story went. Had run away together. Some said they went to a distant family friend of Francis's in Florence. Nobody was certain. But how could Clare elope with Francis when everyone knew – at least the prominent landowners (a medieval mafia, someone said) did – that Lord Ranieri di Bernardo had been chasing her since she was fifteen years of age at every opportunity he got. Who could blame him? If the beautiful statuesque Clare were alive today she would have won the annual Miss Assisi Beauty Pageant hands down. And you know what that means. Fame and glory. It was what Francis had wanted too in his former life.

No, the affair with Ranieri never worked out. He took it badly too. The disappointment was "deep deep", as we say in my side of the world. Actually the last time, the final time they met, Clare gave Ranieri a lesson on the grace of God and tried to persuade him to become religious himself. That's not exactly a turn-on on a date. But it reveals her mind, her character, her youthful determination, her steely single-mindedness as a woman, and her extraordinary resolve to make her own decisions about her own life.

It will be clear from all this that Francis and Clare were *not* detached beings wandering in clouds of holiness. Rather the opposite. Clare's clearly stated life plan, even before she met Francis when she was seventeen years old, was to live in penance and poverty. What comes over a person at such a young age that makes them take decisions like that? People who question society, who hold up a mirror to it, who feel compelled to radically interrogate their own cultures, who consciously decide to walk away from their own social conditioning are in the same company as Mother Theresa, as Karl Marx, Ghandi, Martin Luther King, Nelson Mandela and any other reformer you choose to mention. But she goes beyond that. She is an early example of an extraordinary Christian woman breaking into a male dominated hierarchy and society. Like Teresa of Avila and Catherine of Siena she challenged the social conventions of her time and faced fierce sexism before the word existed. Like Teresa, Catherine and other dynamic women in Christian history she was the architect of a new timeless spirituality which was to inspire millions of women and men for the next eight hundred years. She probably didn't know at the time that with Francis she was shaking global consciousness of religious life. That was Clare from Assisi, the contemporary of Francis. A woman apart, whose time had come. A woman of history and still with many thousands of followers after eight centuries. From the point of woman leadership in the church today often forgotten in the discussion is the fact that there are presently about 800 leader (CEO-like) nuns guiding the destinies of 800,000 religious women scattered across the globe's cultures.

Clare's journey was anything but easy.

It doesn't stop there. Did I say a tough, steely character? Now other women from Assisi wanted to follow her example. They flocked to the convent at San Damiano – including her own sister, Agnes. And Agnes too was something else. Another story that confounds and mystifies. Her leaving home also became a life and death struggle. Literally. Here again the family militia, led by her quick-tempered uncle, Monaldo, fought to bring her home. Damned if they were going to be humiliated again as with her sister, Clare. Inside the door of the convent they tried patient persuasion but failed to convince her to come back to the family where she was assured of prosperity, security and marriage. Pleadingly, she refused. Tempers flared. Confrontation followed. Monaldo, eyes a vicious glint in the candlelight, rushed forward. Tables and seats were knocked over, voices raised, blood-curdling expletives were heard, but to no avail. Falling on the ground, Agnes begged the prayers of her sister Clare. A soldier grabbed her by the hair. And then it happened. She became so heavy, a leaden form, that the soldiers couldn't drag her any further. Her uncle was about to strike her a lethal blow with a steel weapon when he was stopped by severe pain as he raised his arm for the final fatal strike. Stunned, he backed off. Astonished, the guards withdrew in shock, in dismay and disarray. It was a miracle. Better all back off, they felt. Confused they withdrew. They were defeated by the determination of this new young sister and the urgent prayers of Clare to a listening God. On returning to their horses, one of the soldiers discovered he was still holding a tuft of Agnes's hair.

If Monaldo had killed Agnes, would they have called it an honour killing – just as we have it today in some countries of the Middle East – to protect the reputation and good name of the family? Would custom have obliged Clare and Agnes's parents to accept the death of their daughter at the hands of her uncle, and in such violent circumstances? Even today uncles are key figures in negotiating the welfare and future of families in many parts of the world. How long ago did eighteen-ish-year-olds start to defy their parents, to run away from home? The answers to these legitimate questions were soon to come, if in a very roundabout way. Young people sometimes show the way to parents. So often where I live in South Africa teenagers become Catholics, followed later by their elders. It breaks all the rules because, while these youngsters are in preparation to become Catholics, they have no Catholic support at home for what they are learning at the church in catechism classes. Something similar was happening in the Offreduccio family. Less violent, less traumatic but sensational all the same. The youngest generation had seen the light.

More of the family, including Clare and Agnes's mother, Ortolana, later joined Francis and his growing movement. The news that Francis and Clare had gone AWOL, had abandoned the nobility and the business sectors of Assisi, soon filtered through the countryside. The bishop's palace was inundated with concerned inquiries – sometimes angry ones too. The rich and famous were upset. The moneyed classes wanted answers.

What did Christ say about bringing a sword to the world, not peace...?

The pressure on Clare was great. As time went on she began to realise that she was in the initial stages of founding an Order in the Church – one that would soon be referred to as "the Poor Clares". She did not know what lay ahead. But she knew and trusted that a loving God would support her – she had seen evidence of that already. She knew she was in the best of company. The stubborn determination of a founder. A female founder-leader in a patriarchal society. And she will give the Pope, Innocent V1, no peace until he accepts her conditions for her new style of religious life.

You don't tell a pope what to do.

But Clare, the woman of the age, did just that – and got away with it. Rome was seriously worried about her. As in the case of Francis, the church authorities wanted her to join an already existing Order of nuns. A messenger was urgently dispatched from the Pope to order Clare by Papal Decree to gather her sisters and join the Benedictine nuns in the district! She refused point-blank. Refused the Pope. Can you blame the Pope for his reaction? For in her rule, which was close to the heart of Francis, she had written that all Franciscans are the same and equal: men and women! This is 1216, eight hundred years before the dignity and equality of women became a global issue.

Clare also clashed with the Pope over the issue of property. Property was everything. Her earlier proposed marriage had been meant to consolidate property transfers. But she had disposed legally of the property she would have inherited. The Church wanted sisters to own property so as to have an income. Clare said no; instead they would support themselves by their own labour. Here were women, nuns called sisters, coming together to create a new economic system, an alternative way of life in the thirteenth century. This was a time when many great thinkers and renowned theologians wondered whether women had souls at all; whether they were a divine mistake or even "failed conceptions". In the San Damiano Convent in Assisi, Clare struggled with the Church for forty years for acceptance and recognition. Yes, forty years.

One day in 1253, Pope Innocent 1V was passing Assisi and, hearing that Clare was dying, decided to call on her. "Is there anything I can do for you?" he asked. "Approve the rule," she responded weakly. "So be it," he wrote at the bottom of the page. It was done. Like Simeon the temple-minder, she could now truly depart in peace. Meanwhile Francis had been overseas for nearly a year in the Middle East and North Africa. He too was making waves and creating more Church history. He was a founder about to become a missionary. And he was the first founder to send others on missions, and to write missionary outreach into the rule of an Order.

A question: What does this story tell us about the power of positive, spirit-led relationships? Think of what St Paul said:
We felt so devoted to you, that we would have been happy to share with you not only the Gospel of God, but also our own lives, so dear had you become. (*1 Thessalonians 2:8*)

PART 2

ST FRANCIS AND JIHAD

Why should we think that Francis of Assisi, 'Gods Fool', the saint who begged for food, cleaned lepers and preached to the birds, has anything to teach us about peacemaking, interreligious dialogue or diplomacy in our dangerous world? Sainthood and statecraft hardly seem to go together in our age, or in any age – *Dr Scott M. Thomas, Department of Economics and International Development, University of Bath, UK. From The Tablet, 7 October 2006*

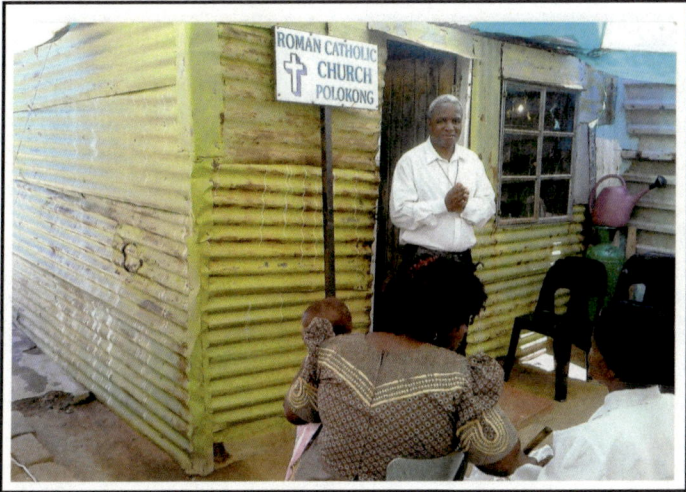

Roman Catholic Church Polokong

A Franciscan prays in a secluded cave used by St Francis as a meditation room

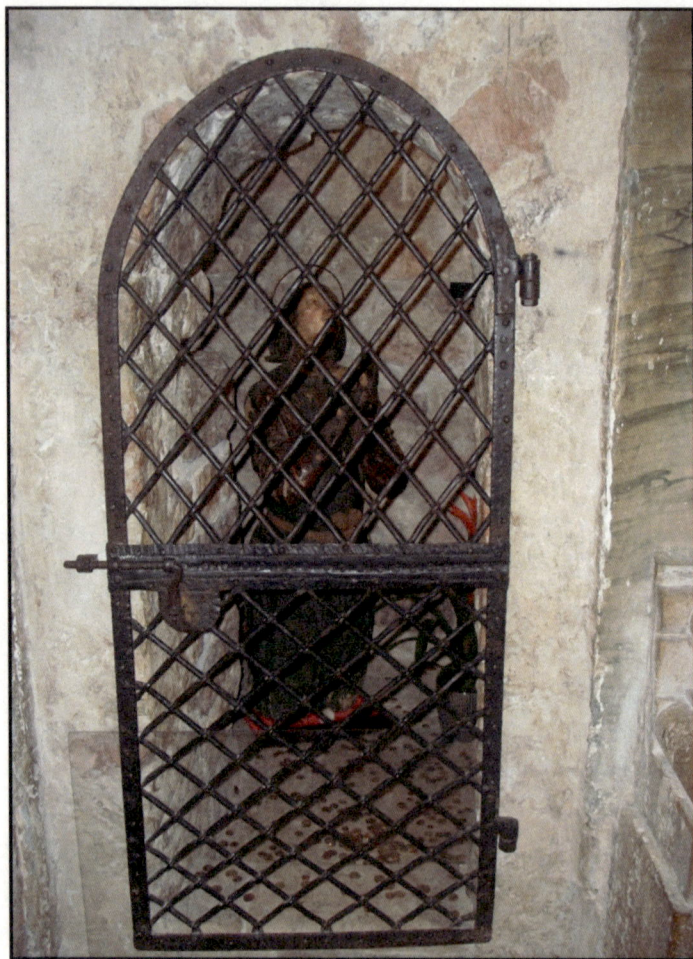

Photo: Bente Wolf Assisi Mission, Italy

The family cell where Francis was imprisoned by his harassed parents. This was common even in the civilised world at that time; today, they would be arrested for child abuse.

Chapter 7

Francis at the Coalface of International Politics

I cannot imagine St Francis of Assisi
talking about rights – *Simone Weil* (*1943*)

You have to admire Francis's singular determination,
even daring, at the frontiers of international politics. The
violence of war did not deter him from doing what he
believed was right. His growing relationship with the
Christ of the vulnerable compelled him to travel far and
wide in pursuit of reconciliation and peace-building in
the Body of Christ not only in the Italy of that time but
beyond, even beyond Europe.

Today, based on our turbulent pastoral
experiences in the final days of apartheid in South Africa,
we would call what Francis was doing "crisis ministry".
As I write, the Christian churches of the Middle East and
parts of Africa are discovering what "crisis ministry" is all
about. It is a service or parish ministry you quickly
develop by trial and error when your world goes into
sudden meltdown or explodes in your face; a ministry of
presence and accompaniment with people when there is
little else to hope for. In the Middle East we hope and
pray they will make the right decisions, based on
prayerful discernment and wise interventions, based on
options for the poor and the example and spirit of St
Francis.

Francis's understanding of the Gospel when applied to life was clearly different from that of the Paris-educated Pope Innocent III. At that time, incidentally, the Pope was a sort of executive president of all Europe, as much a politician as a theologian and shepherd of souls. It was under Innocent's jurisdiction, incidentally, that the Fourth Lateran Council began to use the word "transubstantiation" formally and decreed, as well, that Catholics must confess once a year and receive Holy Communion at Easter, in a state of grace. It tried to move the clergy away from being merely "mass priests". Interestingly, this Council had a child protection clause against the secret marriages of minors common and customary at the time. This child abuse still survives in non-Christian areas of our world.

But Pope Innocent, who was only thirty-seven when elected, had the wisdom to understand the Francis phenomenon. He liked the man. Francis's group, he noted, was different than the other sects and cults mushrooming all over Europe. To be fair, Pope Innocent III had a dream (remember the life-changing dreams surrounding the birth of Jesus) in which he saw St Francis propping up the Lateran Basilica and interpreted it to mean that new orders of friars (Franciscan and Dominicans) would render valuable service to the church). So he accepted Francis's first rule.[1] He began to see that the little man from the mountains of the interior had a message that was needed for the whole of Christendom. Curiously at first, he welcomed the

---

[1] The first "'Rule" (now lost) on which the Franciscan order was based.

religious beggar who might be challenging a way of life in Europe that was built on wealth and power.

Francis, now the religious revolutionary, was showing a system of sharing, caring, simplicity and community, without property and power as an alternative way of life. Cardinal Joseph Ratzinger many years ago said of Francis's conviction: "Francis's no to that type of church [power, lordships, dukes, excellencies, wealth] could not be more radical. It is what we would call a prophetic protest." A person with right-wing leanings today might, on the other hand, call it a "socialist pipedream".

Later, historians were to acknowledge that the formation of Francis's Order, which was already known as the Lesser Brothers, was a turning point in Christian attitudes towards wealth, simplicity, poverty and authority. Coupled with humility this lack of power, wealth or social privilege was the secret weapon Francis was soon to bring to the negotiating table in a Middle Eastern conflict.

Pope Francis is acutely aware of all this and wants to appropriate the same gift in his own ministry.

Chapter 8

Francis Creates a Stir in Africa

Francis's life was lived on the road –
Murray Bodo and Susan Saint Sing: A
Retreat with Francis and Clare

In previous chapters we saw that Francis was developing and living a new kind of spirituality. All this time – not deliberately, not with studied foresight – he had been building up a completely new relationship with God, with himself, with the friars, with the poor, with civil society, and finally with all things. In a sense he had gone beyond recall. Now he was breathing new structures into consecrated life. The ecclesiastical authorities couldn't keep up with him. They hoped, in vain, that he would settle for the monastic life. But Francis was on the move: a vow of stability was definitely not on his agenda.

More was to follow. He wasn't finished with his very public apostolate. He wasn't finished with his peacemaking. He wasn't finished with his political interventions. He wasn't finished his travelling for Christ. He was about to embark on a more extreme and dangerous pastoral initiative. A first-time missionary project, something the founder of an Order had never done before. Francis would probably have claimed he was guided by the Holy Spirit. Anyway he prevailed upon a Chapter of the early friars to grant him permission to go to the Holy Land. Could they refuse? His knowledge of the workings of the Holy Spirit was uncomplicated. It sent his brothers at times scurrying into disbelieving huddles. There must have been consternation at this Chapter meeting – it's not impossible that it would have nearly collapsed; such was the fervour and passion at play. Were you ever at the early meetings of a new Order? Did Francis foolishly want martyrdom even before his Order was properly established? Many wondered with great anxiety was he walking away from, perhaps even trying to escape, his religious problems? What would happen to their new Order? And what would happen to Clare's new Order? All very distressing. They were being left as orphans, the more timid thought. Would there be struggles within the brotherhood that could bring disarray and perhaps even ruin?

Many of the brothers found it difficult to understand him. To understand his logic. He was in a world of his own most of the time, they thought. So often on the move. The friars were numbed especially those coming from professional and business backgrounds. There was no business plan, no consolidation of the new Order, no planning committees for the expansion of the new fraternity. Wall Street would have cringed. He claimed that God was sending him to the Holy Land or the Middle East or someplace remote. Wow!

His leave-taking from his parents at their shop in Assisi was tense, and silent and sad. He found his mother and brother, Angelo chatting with some customers. His father was away on a business trip in, where else, France. Implicit and unspoken in the visit was the fact that he might never return. His mother was broken hearted but tried to be brave. He left home returned to the brothers the next morning with a heavy heart. The neighbours saw him off with a certain amount of apprehension. A week later he packed his rags and set off with one of the more agreeable brothers, Brother Illuminato. No travel agents or renewal of passports in those days. They were off to Egypt, the land where the Holy Family had once lived as refugees. It was a long walk, a treacherous and arduous journey, but a time of grace too. Probably a sort of sabbatical for the two of them, for it gave them time to discuss the recent meeting of all the friars from which they were coming and to think about what might lie ahead. They set off on a journey halfway across the world, in search of something. Who knew what? A dream, a place far away that needed peace.

Needless to say, those who had joined his Order to flee the world didn't follow him. His departure made them wonder if they had joined the right Order. Some, frightened by his constant gallivanting, left and joined the Benedictines, where they would find more stability! It was a long time to be away from home too. Was he even anticipating returning at all? The boat voyage, via Cyprus, gave Francis plenty of time to ponder the strange direction his life was taking, including the unplanned founding of a new type of Order within the church. And he wondered what was ahead. He was on a mission – his third – this time to the followers of Mohammed, crossing the seas once crossed by Paul of Tarsus. That precious historical footnote quietly confirmed his determination.

Francis, as we will see, was not too interested in the big issue of the Church at that time, namely the liberation of the Holy Land. He did, however, influence it as we shall see. He had other ideas. Liberation and war did not feature in his thoughts now. It was his personal desire to meet, not to fight, the leaders of the Islamic world. He knew that he had been sent to engage non-Europeans rather than to visit places. Sent to meet people rather than to conquer new lands. If he seemed to have no plan for the brothers he left at home he had a plan now. His plan was to use the Church's Crusade armies camped outside the strategically important Muslim city of Damietta in the Nile delta and to hop, skip and jump his way into the Muslim camp.

One early humid Tuesday morning – 9 September 1219 – during a year-long lull in the attack on the Muslims forces in North Africa, Francis made his move, his peace and reconciliation move. When he arrived at Damietta from Syria, Francis was welcomed into the crusader camp by the French bishop, Jacques de Vitry, who was fascinated by his arrival, and by his tramp like appearance. A wandering "monk" type, of which there were many these days, he had heard about this man including that his father, a textile merchant, used to visit France on business matters. However, the military chaplains, especially the ostentatious Cardinal Pelagio Galvani, (an appointee of Pope Honorius III, with military, yes military, ambitions[2]) were uneasy, even sceptical of Francis's sudden arrival. They wondered what he was up to. This was no place for drifter mendicants, they thought. He wasn't even a priest, some whispered. These were hawkish, theologically conservative clerics,

---

[2] Galvani has gone down in history as having made a bad decision in turning down al-Kamil's peace offers.

unaccustomed to the unpredictable ways of prophets. Francis could feel the tension. They were on opposite sides, clearly, and listening to their questions, Francis realised that they were worlds apart. The bishops were not sure how to handle the situation. They knew that Francis was known personally to the Pope. A reason for caution. And it was humiliating for a cardinal and other prelates to be upstaged by a former playboy, no matter how reformed he was.

Francis and his companion rested for a few days and took in the situation before them. They still had their doubts about all this. Why was God asking this of them? Their trek to the frontiers was now over. Their own private thoughts intensified as they saw what lay before them. Their beloved home province of Umbria was but a distant memory. They wondered would they ever see it again. They talked and prayed for more clarity. They were probably in a state of readiness for any eventuality, even death, and would have made the appropriate preparations with the army chaplains. Quietly they knew they might not be coming back – like astronauts today going to the edge of space or even for a landing beyond.

In the war zone Francis was appalled at what he saw. He had immediate flashbacks to his own personal horrific experiences on the battlefields of Perugia. It probably helped him cope somewhat with the situation. It was certainly worse than he had expected. He saw everywhere injured and dying soldiers being tended to. He was told of bloodshed and devastation, of merciless horror, looting and unforgettable brutality. A wasteland of blood orgy, despair and death. And here in Africa he saw soldiers crazed by the merciless heat of the desert sun. The First World War trenches were like the siege of Damietta in the time of the Fifth Crusade except replace the rivers of mud with a scorching desert sun. But there was no backing out now. He had to do what he had come to do. It was a divine long-term summons to pastoral intervention which no doubt his begrudgers called a naive and attention-seeking flirt with notoriety. After all he had been sent by no church authority and that for most was paramount. In fact it was the crusaders who had church authority behind them not him. Startled, bleary-eyed crusader troops awoke one morning to the rumour that the two mendicants from Assisi had vanished into no man's land and had been captured by the Islamic forces. "What madness is this?" they asked when they heard the news. Somebody should have stopped them from going over there. Heads would roll, they knew.

What would the Holy Father say when he heard of this seemingly treasonous behaviour? Deny Francis the plenary indulgence (a special way to Paradise) promised to all decent hardworking God-fearing Muslim-killing crusaders? Or even close his Order, perhaps! In fact, privately, Francis might have had doubts about indulgences for crusaders. He had already received his own Portiuncula Indulgence[3] from the Pope – much to the displeasure of the cardinals, who had anxiously

------

[3] In a small chapel in Portiuncula, near Assisi, Francis had a vision of the Blessed Virgin telling him to ask whatever favour he desired. In what became known as the Portiuncula Indulgence, he asked that all those who came there to pray for forgiveness would receive pardon for all their sins.

explained to His Holiness that "it will undermine the indulgences we are granting the crusaders". But Francis, encouraged by a vision of the Blessed Trinity and the Mother of God, was happy that a person could have their sins forgiven, not, as formerly, only by going on a Crusade, but simply by a prayerful visit to the church of St Mary of the Angels on the lowlands below Assisi. So much for Francis's direct non-violent interventions in political and papal affairs. But what was the aftermath to be? The repercussions for himself and the church?

For Christianity, indeed?

Chapter 9

St Francis and "Osama Bin Laden"

"Blessed", Jesus says, "are the peacemakers, for they shall be called the children of God." Consider carefully that it is not the people who call for peace but those who make peace who are commended
– St Bernard of Clairvaux

After two weeks of amazing, eye-opening spiritual discussions with Sultan Malek al-Kamil, a nephew of the great Saladin of history who defeated the Third Crusade, Francis and Brother Illuminato set out for home. The Sultan had been absolutely intrigued by this most unassuming Christian who didn't even carry a weapon. He had even given Francis a gift, a medieval vuvuzela – an ivory horn, the only record of the visit. The Crusade soldiers were understandably shocked by Francis's behaviour. What had happened over there, they wanted to know. Was he a sell-out, they wondered. Perhaps even a spy of some sort. Was he going to tell them to lay down their arms and make peace? Would he give them a report back?

He seemed to like the Muslims, the sworn enemies of the Cross. How *could* he? Had he not seen the bloodshed, the devastation? Many thought he had been brainwashed while with the enemy. Radicalised, like what has happened today with some young people going to

Syria to fight for Islamic State. Perhaps they were right, for he had returned to the Crusade camp completely unharmed – and changed even. If he was alive today Intelligence services would have him on their danger lists. Francis and Brother Illuminato for their part were overwhelmed by the reception they received. They had been to the vortex of the clash of civilisations. They had been extremely moved to see Muslim soldiers praying five times a day. The Christian soldiers barely prayed at all.

But there were other questions blowing in the wind in the aftermath of Francis's visit to the Islamic leaders. Questions the Christian generals were asking their chaplains. Think about it. What, we might well ask with them, possessed Francis to ignore so openly the wishes of the Holy See in this whole episode? St Bernard of Clairvaux had preached the Papal Crusade with the words, "When the knight of Christ kills the malefactor, his act is not homicide but, if one can use the expression, 'malecide'; he is in all and for all the agent of Christ's vengeance on those who commit evil." That was the religious and devotional climate of the time. Not so very different from what we see in militant Islam today. Francis was going beyond this thinking, going further than the Church, crossing new pastoral and religious divides, because he was inspired to do so. Is it this that Pope Francis finds so attractive about him? From that day, after he arrived back from talking to the Sultan, the "holy man of Assisi" was seen by the military high command as a liability, a *persona non grata*. Indeed, a "loose cannon" needing to be watched.

In the light of global developments since the September 2001 attack on the United States, it seems that the world could do with a few more loose cannons of the Francis type to defuse political pressure points across the globe. Quietly, Francis was overwhelmed by his own recent actions in northern Egypt, at Damietta on the Nile: his sheer audacity, his strange courage, his childlike daring, his amazing trust in God. What he had done was like having a private meeting with Stalin in Moscow or Islamic State (Isis) in Iraq. Or the unlamented Osama Bin Laden.

Most of his contemporaries agreed, however, that Francis was a fool. They couldn't understand, in today's language, his cutting edge hands-on ministry whether it was public peacemaking, abandoning himself to meditation in the wilderness or founding an Order.

But who would understand it even today?

Chapter 10

Francis Ignores the Papal War Machine

God's glory has not been spread by force and weapons, but by poor fishermen – *Savonarola (1452–1498)*

Peace is the only battle worth waging – *Albert Camus*

To put it in a political context: Francis was caught up in a war not of his making. He was doing a United Nations thing before its time. Uninvited. He was exploring peace and love and solutions *during* a vicious war between cultures and religions, not after a war as is usual. His body language was telling. His total lack of affectation or attitude sometimes called humility carried the day. Such a thing had never been done before. Besides, peace talks are supposed to take place *after* a war. Religious discussions never. Not during a battle on the killing fields. It would have been seen as distracting, perhaps a ploy deliberatively concocted by the Christians to fool the Muslim forces. To catch them unawares. That's how different and dangerous it was. It was totally crazy and unorthodox in human terms. Think of Syria or Libya in our time.

A few weeks after Francis's conversations with the Muslim leader, the Christians killed seventy-eight thousand Muslims! That was seventy-eight thousand plenary indulgences for the crusaders! (Heaven was stormed with saved souls those days. The sudden tsunami of Christian soldiers left St Peter reeling. And to make matters more confusing there were Muslims among them too). But the tide was turning. Soon, with patience, and as the Christian armies grew weary for one reason or another, the Muslims began to get the upper hand. In fact two years later the now defeated crusaders abandoned Damietta. This brought the age of the crusaders to an inglorious end.

Eight hundred years later, in 2004, Pope John Paul apologised to Muslims for the bloody history of the Crusades. Do Muslims also need to go on record apologising for their own atrocities and the despoiling of the Holy Places in times gone by? So Francis of Assisi was right after all. He had done the right thing but it was completely misunderstood at the time. He was eight hundred years before his time. The powers that be were eight hundred years behind the times! God protect us from leaders who do not submit to the guidance of the Holy Spirit but rather draw on their own human cleverness and resources.

Francis had just launched a new kind of interfaith dialogue. A new way of evangelising. A way which respected other cultures and religions for the goodness found in them. A way that built trust between peoples. A way that started with people not doctrine. But how often has this whole episode been lost to the "distortions and stereotype images" of the official biographers![4] St Francis's spirituality seemed to nourish his gift for proactive non-violent interventions in theatres of conflict near and far. This simple, pastoral, spontaneous strategy

---

[4] The words of Raphael Bonanno, OFM.

and spirituality is rare in religious leadership today. In fact, among distinguished European commentators, the Damietta episode has been considered a failure for Francis, because it did not lead to his martyrdom or, especially, the conversion of the Muslim leader. For Christianity at the time, Francis's visit to Damietta was an embarrassment. A field day for his detractors. Not so as seen today. No less a source than *Time* magazine[5] agrees that Francis's unique dialogue approach at the time "could be a useful paradigm for a frank and sincere dialogue in an ever turbulent religious world".

In a general audience in early 2009, Pope Benedict pointed out the importance of this period in the life of St Francis: "I want to underline this episode in the life of St Francis because of its great relevance. At a time when there was a conflict between Christianity and Islam, Francis – armed only with his faith and his personal meekness – successfully followed the path of dialogue." Today, pioneered against all odds by St Francis, dialogue is the universally accepted solution to conflict. Former British Prime Minister Tony Blair and former American President Jimmy Carter travel the world promoting this solution in relation to world peace. Professor Hans Küng, president of the Global Ethic Foundation, writes:

No peace among the nations
    without peace among the religions.
No peace among the religions
    without dialogue between the religions.

---

[5] 27 November 2006.

No dialogue between the religions
   without global ethical standards.
No survival of our globe
   without a global ethic.

There is another interesting point of history here; a fruit of Francis's brief Islamic ministry in North Africa. After the Crusade campaigns, the Church was obliged to reassess its evangelising strategies. Military solutions had failed; something else was needed. Something lasting and acceptable to all sides. Another way.

One unexpected and more immediate outcome of this event comes to mind.

In 1342 the Pope asked the Franciscans to be guardians of the holy places on behalf of Christendom. And today Franciscans care for the holy places in the non-Christian countries of the Middle East. This came as a direct result of Francis's ministry in Egypt.

From Africa, Francis eventually set sail for home. On the return journey he talked at length with Brother Illuminato about their recent amazing encounters. They had experienced so much; they had seen so much; and they had learned so much about their Church and about the "others", the feared Saracens. And they had come out of it alive! They were on the way home. It certainly had been one of the most daring, dangerous and fearless Christian missionary operations (we will call it "Operation Jesus") in history. Not planned in Joint Operation Headquarters in the Pentagon. No night visors or sophisticated weaponry were necessary for safe passage. Even the highly-trained tactical combatants, the Navy

Seals, would concede that this surely was outside their competence and abilities!

He wondered what flak he would get when he got home. What he had just done was by normal sensible standards outrageous, unheard of, and very unpopular. Meeting the Islamic leader had not been planned, expected, or anticipated by anyone. Francis had gone against all informal opinion polls of the time. Everyone was against what he had done: the Muslims, the Christians, the Franciscans, the Benedictines, the people of Assisi, his parents and family, his friends at home, the politicians, the Germans, the church and clergy, even the Pope. So when Francis met Malek al-Kamil he represented no one, neither Pope nor King. He was alone in the desert. What manner of man can be so sure of himself and so defiant of public opinion? His occupying the world stage for those few weeks at Damietta was beyond comprehension to all who knew him. But perhaps he wasn't as organised as I've made it sound. I bet he was full of doubts, paradoxes, ambiguities, confusions and contradicting impulses. Perhaps he made these very human qualities normal and noble. Yes, he had much to think about on the way home.

Their new consciousness, their new awareness of the complexity of God's world was almost beyond Francis and Brother Illuminato. They needed space to absorb it all. He hadn't gone to Egypt with a programme. A programme to make converts, to make peace and even to seek martyrdom. If that was the plan, it failed. Or did it? I would like to suggest that his pastoral approach was what we today call a "ministry of presence". A Christian and church presence is vitally important in all situations of conflict, even today. During apartheid, especially in its final years when the old political system was unbundling, unpacking and generally falling apart on the streets of South Africa, the ministry of pastoral presence and accompaniment took on a new meaning. Ministers and priests constantly gathered community leaders together for crisis consultations, interpreting events daily with the people, organising community funerals after massacres and police killings, actively monitoring arrests, supporting treason trialists, and generally being a public sign of hope and a shepherding presence on the streets. Monitoring society from our Christian perspective drew church people into a deeper spiritual togetherness, which has endured to this today. Pope Francis vividly describes this ministry of presence in this way: "What is necessary is proximity: to embrace, kiss, touch, hug a son or a daughter. When the Church neglects this proximity, it is like a mother who communicates with her son [only] in a letter."

After weeks of travelling, Francis and Brother Illuminato arrived back in their homeland. His religious brothers and the sisters of Clare were overjoyed. At home, Francis continued to serve his new Order but with a changed perspective, a broader insight and a newly enlightened understanding of the way things work in the world. His body, however, was weakening and his eyes were troubling him. The burden of his "extreme" ministry was beginning to tell. Besides, he had now received the stigmata of the Lord on his frail body. This divine event, showing God's favour and Francis's love of the Cross and passion of the Saviour, happened after he had been back at home for some time, when he was at La Verna, making a retreat (a time of withdrawal from everyday life to enter into closer communion with God).

Here was something of profound significance.

Was God giving divine approval to Francis's evangelising mission to the Muslim world by appearing to him at the moment of the stigmata as a crucified seraph (angel) – the only time this has happened in history? For it is recorded that Mohammed, during his religious experiences, had asked God to show Himself under the form of an angel. Perhaps this is why the angel in the vision to Francis on Mount La Verna was the crucified Christ. Islam with Christianity. Was this appearance of a crucified angel meant to lead Muslims to the crucified Christ, and was Francis to be their intercessor? Was the receiving of the La Verna stigmata a response to Francis's Damietta pilgrimage? Indeed did Islam "provoke" the apparition of the stigmata at La Verna?[6] If so, it somehow draws Islam into the world of Christian mysticism, which could be game-changing for the troubled relations between Islam and Christianity.

The implications are breathtaking.

---

[6] For this thought I'm indebted to the twentieth century (Catholic) Islamic scholar Louis Massignon.

Chapter 11

What Francis Learned from Islam

> The Western world may have achieved
> remarkable advances in science and
> technology, but this does not say that its
> moral and spiritual life in theory and in
> practice is better than that of all other
> cultures – *Bonaventure Hinwood, OFM*
> (*Southern Cross, 18–24 March 2015*)

But Francis didn't see it like that. He felt carried by
something bigger than himself. It was mystical. And he
felt it all over himself. His new awareness, his new
awakening, arising from his startling meeting with the
leader of Islam, showed him that God was active in non-
Christian faiths too. Even today we are struggling to
understand this. Pope Francis has washed the feet of
Muslims. Francis's eyes were opened in new ways to God.
It astonished him that Muslims had ninety-nine names
for God that they invoked, using beads, (precursor of the
Rosary prayer) all the time. It astonished him that they
were a praying army. That Muslims prayed five times a
day! It was a real discovery. His own praise of God
deepened even more. He was willing to learn from non-
Christians; in this case, the enemy of all Christendom.
His brothers baulked at this when he got home, and the
clergy he met later cringed. He had lost it, they lamented.
According to history, this Christian "jihad" (holy war) of
the Crusades Alliance failed.

The Islamic Sufi experience was a major jolt to Francis's understanding of mission, of religion, and of the world. Sufi are spiritual Muslims of a mystical order. The encounter with them actually changed him. Encounters do change people. They are good for human relations. They open the doors of people's hearts (a theme of the Year of Mercy) and trust and friendship begins to pick up, catch on, deepen and flourish. The Islamic Sultan was a very enlightened leader of the time. (Some Sufi authorities even today claim St Francis as one of their own in the spirit of Rumi, a medieval Sufi mystic. It's not so surprising then when in 2015 a group of Sufi related dancers – "Swirling Dervishes" – were invited to Rome by Istanbul Franciscans to an interreligious prayer meeting called in the "Spirit of Assisi"). As a Sufi sympathiser it was relatively easy for the leader of the Muslim armies to have spiritual conversations with a powerless Christian nobody, a humble Christian nomad and his friend. But during a war! And two weeks of religious discussions during a lull in the violence and bloodshed. No wonder it still mystifies most commentators.

If I could bring in my own experiences of the South African theatre when apartheid society was at its most violently defensive just before it started to crack and go into free fall. St Francis sitting with the enemy reminds me of when we pastors were obliged to sit with the enemy during the final days of crumbling apartheid in the eighties. I served on African delegations representing local resistance groups (unions, churches, teachers, health professionals) in meetings with the dreaded South African security services. It's extremely difficult to sit at a table across from people who detest you, who spy on you daily, who mastermind regional assassinations, who regularly interrogate and torture detainees about your activities, and who seek reasons to have you deported at the earliest possible time. And all the time you are facing and talking with professional liars, the local security backbone of apartheid.

I didn't have to be there, didn't want to be there.

Then you realise that Francis was there before you. It's a formidable argument. He was the great peacemaker of the medieval period. If Francis could eat with the enemy so could we friars. (Sometimes these meetings involved friars Edward "Teddy" Lennon and Lucas Bambezela). But it was not comfortable.

I try not to glare across the long table at the stoic phalanx of neatly dressed officials representing the different state security organs. We know they have large files on us and believe we white priests on black delegations have betrayed the white race. They are probably God-fearing church-attending members of the Dutch Reformed Church fed on the authoritarian teachings of Calvin by a clergy that for forty years had justified biblically the apartheid divisions of the country. They know that we are illegally living in so-called black areas but at this juncture are weary of making an issue of it. They pretend not to take notice of us but are in fact using the meeting to observe and assess the quality of the opposition community leaders at close quarters. The business sector is also represented and tries to be as neutral as possible when neutrality is not an option as is often the way in situations of conflict.

So when Francis met the Muslims there was more

to it than meets the eye. Many invisible dynamics were at play. They didn't know for instance whether they could trust one another. The Sultan probably thought the Francis party was a delegation from the Crusades which couldn't have been further from the truth. He had to interrogate Francis in order to assure himself they were not mercenaries in disguise, religious fanatics, or double agents. No wonder the conversations went on for two weeks.

It was like meeting Stalin to interest him in Jesus during his dreaded purges at the height of the Cold War. He would have surely thought Francis was a secret American agent and would accordingly have bugged his and Brother Illuminato's rooms in the Kremlin! Francis only realised later that he as a European had been on a learning curve about the religion of Islam. These were life-changing exchanges for all parties. But even during the modern Cold War era the legacy of Francis of peacemaking continues internationally. For example in December 1982 a Franciscan statement, inspired by that great peacemaker himself, Friar Louis Vatale of the California province, was circulated globally calling on governments "to renounce the use of nuclear weapons and to eliminate nuclear arsenals ..."

Should we have expected the Sultan to convert to Christianity? Why? Is that not being small minded showing a lack of knowledge, of understanding in time of great turmoil and war? Tony Blair deliberately waited until after his retirement to convert to Catholicism. If Malek al-Kamil had converted he probably would have been immediately killed by his own leaders (as it was, there had been an attempted coup), a leadership struggle would have followed in the Muslim ranks, Francis would have been killed, and the crusaders would have said "we told you so!"

Fast very forward. Think of this.

Like St Francis who insisted on meeting the leader of Islam, Nelson Mandela also had tea with his former oppressor, President Botha, with his former prosecutor, Percy Yutar who wanted promotion from a successful case against Mandela, and finally paid a courtesy visit to Mrs Verwoerd, the wife of the architect of apartheid.

It was only a few weeks later on the way home that Francis heard that a few inexperienced friars had been beheaded in Morocco.

I sometimes wonder why Western writers on the life and times of St Francis have somehow toned down this extraordinary period – a period when we see Francis clearly decoding the political and social signs of the times, leading to his many interventions in areas of conflict. His insistence on forgiveness and peacemaking, among the most challenging of his teachings, needs to be highlighted and celebrated anew by all who love him. Donald Spoto, one of Francis of Assisi's recent biographers, rightly calls Francis "the first person from the West to travel to another continent with the revolutionary idea of peacemaking". Actually Francis was rethinking the Church's teaching on war and peace. He found himself peace-building when the Church was war-mongering. The Pope had sent the crusaders to war. The only good Muslim was a dead Muslim, he believed. Francis said: Sorry; not so. Not true. But he was nice about it. He wasn't brazen about contradicting the Church's theology of war. He just ignored it. He was rethinking and reshaping the attitudes of his society towards war, peace and security. He was initiating, creating, a Franciscan approach to peacemaking and to interreligious dialogue. He was showing an ability to see seeds of truth everywhere, and in all religions. Pope Francis would concur.

The crusader soldiers, the Pope's army, were too fired up to understand the significance of Francis's actions. They were soldiers after all, not theologians or monks. Besides, military life has no place for non-conformists like Francis. Especially non-conformists under the spell of God.

An unpredictable lot!

And one final question: We now know the daring way Francis encountered Islam in his day. In our world many conflict spots involve Christians and Muslims. Today what creative hope would St Francis bring to a world of Islamophobia, Muslim wars, terrorists, fastest-growing faith in the world, clash of civilisations, burkas, Taliban, Islamic State or Caliphate, anti-West imams and ulamas, Sharia law, common-ground approaches and suicide bombers?

For further information see: www.damiettapeace.org.za
Franciscans International and Franciscans and Dominicans for Human Rights

St Francis receiving the stigmata with the miraculous San Damiano cross in the background.

PART 3

WHO OWNS ST FRANCIS?

Until now, Francis's life and work have been interpreted almost exclusively in terms of Western culture, especially the culture of Assisi and of Italy. We are confident that the African experience of human and religious values can give us new insights in such cherished values as prayer, poverty, "minority", joy, simplicity, fraternal life, and evangelical lifestyle – *John Vaughn, Franciscan Minister General 1983*

Chapter 12

Western Christianity is Still on Trial

In Heaven I would want to meet St Francis
of Assisi – *Nobel Prize winner, Archbishop
Emeritus Desmond Tutu*

From Africa, certainly from South Africa, "going overseas"
usually means going to Britain or America, or at least to
the North Atlantic countries. It's something to be
achieved, somewhere to have been. For the young it
spells sophistication and progress. Seen from the outside,
from down under, Europe and America are faraway
dreams even as they draw closer to us through
globalisation. From the South we have this feeling, this
inkling, that the West tends to revolve around itself. A
great mass of affluence up north, inward looking,
exceedingly self-contained and prosperous; and damn
sharp and smart too. It is so different from our world. It's
full of great technology – but declining faith. Its effluents
pollute the world – especially the developing world – with
consumerism and materialism. Up north they have few
wars these days although in the last century their
nations plunged the earth into two World Wars and
finished the century with a bloody ethnic cleansing free-
for-all after the breakup of Yugoslavia. In some places in
Europe, however, the flame of tribalism still lies not far
below the surface, just waiting to be fanned. Rightfully,
education is still a priority in those lands. They study a
lot. Most of the great Christian centres of education are

located there. Europe is still seen as the seat of Christianity. It is also, may we say, the seat and centre of former colonialism from which many countries are still trying to cope with the arbitrary nature of their foreign made borders. (one thinks of the north/south divide in Ireland). We are one of those countries. We in South Africa.

The Arab world and developing countries see Christianity as Western and European. At least their thinkers do. They see Europe, not the Middle East of Jesus's time, as the home of Christianity. Most people don't realise that Christianity is a non-Western religion which emerged from a subjugated, colonised Jewish people into a subjugated, terrorised Christian people. For its first three hundred years it was officially treated as a dangerous, subversive cult from the eastern Mediterranean. When it was finally legalised, it spread throughout Europe and became a "Western" religion that, according to historians, was used by Westerners to further the aims of colonialism. Up to recent times indeed Christianity has been dominated by Westerners. But that is changing; Africa and Asia are becoming the new centres of Christianity.

All this casts a certain light on Christianity. A certain window on our faith. An angle embedded in and emerging from Western society. Missionaries, sisters, priests, brothers and lay people always carry this awareness from the past, this necessary baggage and heritage. And when they return on leave to Europe or America they know they are back in that Church of their youth. An old Church of ancient buildings that breathes a ministry and life that flourished in past centuries.

Grand old cut stone walls that speak a language of yesteryear and suggest a way of thinking and ministry that may have passed its sell-by date.

In a side street in Vienna, I slip into the Franciscan church and sit alone, surrounded by gold-plated ornate altars, numerous life-size statues, a lofty, elaborately decorated pulpit – all highly evocative of other times and periods in European history. The smell of incense, the ancient silence, the secular and religious intertwined on the walls and balconies. The interior exudes the heavy odour of former days of glory, of majestic liturgies, of organ recitals, visits by renowned composers, military leaders, conquerors, prime ministers. It is much like most great churches in Europe. The deep silence of this ecclesiastical wonderland is broken only by the dull tinkle of an elderly lady's coin in a half-full candle box before the Heaven-facing statue of the wonder-worker St Anthony of Padua.

If I were living in the West and not a returning missionary, I too would have given in, a long time ago, to the nostalgic pressure to conform to ossified theological and pastoral ideas. About what? About life and liturgy. About priorities and principles. About church and choir. About bell, book and candle. Yes, we have seen what Western Christianity has produced. A rich and wonderful faith heritage with an amazing history of saintly witness to the teachings of Christ. And yes, one of the great achievements of the Western Church has been to reach out to the non-Christianised world: again following the teachings of our Saviour.

But alas, on this front too, the old missionary

model of Church is in decline. We are witnessing a fading of the once vigorous missionary global outreach. Clergy going on the missions is no more. I am one of the last of that breed. Thank you Life for the memories. We are living through the slow demise of a centuries-old missionary project. Alas, the day of the Western missionary is over – at least for the time being. Lamented often, even by missionaries themselves. The twenty-first century is turning out to be a very sobering time for the Church. Even a time of despondency, if you are not on your guard.

In fact there is a time for everything. The missionaries have done their work. And their efforts have been blessed by God. That part of the European Church's missionary outreach has been a success – an unqualified success. These missionaries established a new vigorous, living Body of Christ beyond the West. Look beyond the borders of Europe we mention again. Have you noticed what's happening in the Church outside Europe? The new hub of Christianity is where the missionaries quietly laid the foundations over all those years. It is found in the global south, especially in Africa. A slumbering giant, created by missionaries; a religious renaissance awakening down under. Pope Benedict called Africa a spiritual lung for humanity. And this spiritual lung is moving north. Perhaps even to re-evangelise the north. And why not? Leading the migration is Pope Francis and his non-European ways of seeing and of understanding reality. Something new is out there.

St Francis too became an apostle of the deprived and least privileged of our planet – now mostly found in the developing world. In the process he changed everything. He blew the status quo to smithereens. He redefined holiness. He became a religious maverick. He left his "First World" affluent life and went to live in an impoverished "Third World" culture never to look back, never to return home. What happened in Assisi was to mesmerise and influence Christianity for the next 800 years. And like Pope St John Paul, they canonised him *subito*.

Chapter 13

A Question of Eurocentric Saints

Not only are the African saints a gift to the
African Church but also to the Universal
Church – *South African Archbishop Buti
Tlhagale, 2012*

It is an indisputable fact that no single
culture can exhaust the mystery of our
redemption in Christ – *Pope Francis, The
Joy of the Gospel: 118*

Before proceeding I must raise the subject of the saints of
our "Western" Christianity. These wonderful heroes of
Christianity. The ones who walked the talk, our
superstars. Or – for those who lived with them –
"crackpots" who showed that the Gospel could be lived.
There is one thing that has intrigued me in times past
especially living in the developing world. Perhaps you too
have noticed? Holiness seems to be almost monopolised
by the industrialised world. I sometimes wonder did it
start there. And was it exported with the missionaries for
most of our saints come from there. Were there no
indigenous saints? None ever – for all those centuries
before the coming of Christianity? Well, perhaps Saint
Moses in the Old Testament, and the prophets? Were
there no anonymous saints?

Western Catholics have had a virtual monopoly on

saints. Their hard work, education, ambition, devotion and money help to get their Christian heroes memorialised. Made into holy pious pictures for mass distribution. Oh, and all those saints are lily white, Caucasian, in complexion. And look at their sky-blue eyes. Sometimes those who live in the global north seem to sanitise their saints before hoisting them into their lofty stained-glass windows. They tend to put their saints – our saints – nearly out of reach. At least from where I stand. I mean you couldn't imagine them being earthy, complex and subject to temptation.

We in the turbulent southern hemisphere look differently at our holy people. Happily we don't have too many stained-glass windows to which we might banish them. Besides it would be too expensive a plan for a squatter parish. Out of reach really. We like saints who have not only struggled with self-perfection (the Europeans) but also those who lived like us and were people of the soil. Some rare examples: the Ugandan saints, Charles Lwanga and his companions. Today they are world famous African saints, as is the emancipated Arab slave, Josephine Bakhita. Here in South Africa we hope soon to see St Benedict Daswa, South Africa's first martyr. Then there is another Benedict: Benedict the African, whose parents were kidnapped in central Africa in the sixteenth century by Arab slave merchants. Born to African parents in Sicily he became a local Franciscan leader, miracle worker and first canonised African saint.

Indeed the global south must have thousands of uncanonised saints. All missionaries will tell you that. Our parishes are flooded with saints, both living and dead. Catholics here don't, however, have the resources, energy, money and know-how to promote their saints' causes as public role models for future generations. Our thousands of unrecognised saints were people who lived disadvantaged lives and, like Francis of Assisi, knew poverty and serfdom. Though unlike with Francis, probably not from choice. It's true that we in the South can relate to those saints who faced poverty and slavery and child abuse – saints such as the Uganda martyrs, Bernadette, Patrick and Maria Goretti. We can relate to them because what they experienced still happens today, in our very parishes. We have something in common too with those saints who integrated politics, faith and spirituality in a unique way: people like Simon the Zealot, Thomas More, King Louis of France, Francis Taylor the sixteenth century Lord Mayor of Dublin, and France's own St Joan of Arc.

Context matters too, as we shall see. Thomas More became St Thomas More in a decidedly unecumenical period in English history. In fact Christianity seemed to be breaking up rather than uniting in his time. And the man behind the rupture was none other than Martin Luther himself. St Thomas More fumed, it is recorded, and used extremely unsaintly language in denouncing Brother Luther as "an ape, an arse, a drunkard, a lousy little friar, a piece of scruff, a pestilential buffoon, a dishonest liar." In more modern times we note the solemn beatification of the Austrian farmer, Franz Jagerstatter, who was beheaded by the Nazis because he refused to fight for Hitler. A lay objector with a conscience, who felt betrayed at the time by the silence of his priests and bishops. In South Africa in the 1980s he would have had more support from the bishops. Yes, the global south can relate to these types of saints.

It is a positive sign, a sign of greater, deeper and more inclusive discernment in Rome when we begin to hear of saints emerging from political struggles. Cardinal Camillo Ruini, Vicar General of Rome, in formally opening the diocesan phase of the canonisation process for Fr Luigi Sturzo, founder of the Italian Popular Party, remarked, "precisely because he was a priest, he considered it an obligation to exercise his priestly ministry in a field [party politics] which, while different from the norm, was no less important." Fr Sturzo, he said, had dedicated himself to politics "in order to lead it to its natural aim of charity and service". There are mixed opinions on this understanding of priests in party politics. It's frowned on by the Catholic Church, even, where priests sometimes had much non-Catholic and non-Christian support, often in environments generally hostile to the Church. Of course a priest being in a political party could be divisive in a parish. It's just not practical. It could split the community. But is it as simple as that? During South Africa's transition from dictatorship to democracy, we friars, as ministers of the Gospel, were forced to reappraise our ministry role. We found ourselves in critical and crisis situations almost daily. We were launched, if not catapulted, into a ministry of service previously quite unknown to church authorities and religious leaders. During riots, police killings and trials our churches became emergency community meeting places, clinics and sites where the wounded were cared for and information gathered. This crisis ministry, for that is what it was, of living daily in life-threatening situations, drew us into an alternative sense or understanding of what it was to be religious and a priest. And, as with the disciples after the Resurrection, new openings for evangelisation emerged from these desperate situations.

The churches in South Africa are proud of the Christian roots of the main political party called the African National Congress (ANC) and in general of the Christian background to the politics of the country. This in spite of the fact that hundreds of members of the present South African government were trained and educated in the former communist countries of the Soviet Union and eastern Europe. Some even became atheists in the process. So if we are to learn from history, it would seem that church ministers and priests being involved in politics, even party politics, can have benefits. Prominent leaders in the early ANC were practising church ministers who saw little conflict between their chosen paths. In fact they saw them as different sides of one vocation. Here there can be positive, unthought-of, unforeseen outcomes which serve historic evangelisation. A former Vice-President of South Africa, Kgalema Motlanthe, puts it this way:

> Social justice partly traces its origins in the African National Congress to the religious, especially Christian, vision espoused by early African nationalism. Most of the men and women who would play an immense role in the evolving ideological coherence of the ANC drew inspiration from Christian tradition (*Sunday Times*, 9 November 2014)

But wise, informed, church leaders from the First World who have a sense of the history of the developing world are rare. And that is one reason why they are constantly surprised that Christianity is on the rise in the southern hemisphere.

Chapter 14

Resistance Saints and Political Holiness

A saint is one who makes goodness attractive – *Laurence Housman (1865–1959)*

Mairead Maguire has been clearly influenced by Christian mystics, singling out St Francis and St Clare of Assisi – *The Irish Catholic Sept 4, 2014 on Maguire, 1976 Nobel Peace Prize winner with Betty Williams*

There are other nuances too that people of the South are asking to be aired. I ask the question: Could a soldier, a freedom fighter or leader of heroic resistance to structural sin or oppressive structures ever be canonised in the Catholic Church? People whose resistance to evil might even have led to "collateral damage?" Saints who were in the military, like St Francis of Assisi and Ignatius of Loyola, and who perhaps killed for their cause. St Joan of Arc indeed. Nelson Mandela even! But alas, Mandela was not a Catholic. Besides he claimed he wasn't a saint: "I was a sinner who kept on trying". And, like the prophets of old themselves, he shunned the idea of being seen as a modern-day prophet.

Somehow we are accustomed to believe that the chosen way of life or behaviour of these soldiers of Christ is outside the domain of holiness, the scope of sainthood.

Their type of selfless sacrifice has not been viewed as spiritual. But what if freedom fighters brought peace, justice, harmony and reconciliation to millions? What if they brought freedom of religion to a nation? Does our God not notice? Is peace, harmony, justice and reconciliation not the constant appeal of Our Lady of Medjugorje? Before he resigned, Pope Benedict XVI called it "political holiness". It has always been zealous people who have promoted the cause of saints. Often their spirituality is strongly devotional and personal. One morning while I was unvesting in an Italian sacristy, a little man with a Hitler moustache gently touched me on the shoulder and asked me to sign a petition to have a local holy man canonised. When I emerged from the alb he was gone, but it had been a near thing.

Promoters of the cause of saints work from their particular, mostly Eurocentric social framework and background. Their research, the written records they collect, are usually easily available and accessible. Without records, massive chunks of history go missing. That is why, unlike with the trans-Atlantic slave trade, there are no records of trans-Saharan slavery, which went on much longer because the Arab merchants kept few records. Again, in Europe, candidates for sainthood were for the most part educated. They knew how to read and write. In our part of the planet, history is very often transmitted orally. Records of "great historic events" are barely noted, never mind kept. It is in this vein, as mentioned earlier we wish South Africa's candidate for sainthood, Benedict Daswa, the very best. Yes, there is movement. Benedict, who died fighting witchcraft, was beatified on September 13, 2015. But even in the Western world, where the cult of saints is a long tradition, there remain questions around the Church's choice of saints. Why are the staunchly Catholic, sexually active, and prayerful mothers and fathers of priests, brothers and sisters the world over so obviously absent from the calendar of the Blesseds and Saints? Do we have to be male, celibate, prudish and ordained in order to become saints?

But back to our narrative. People involved in social transformation are seldom considered for sainthood. Often they don't fit into traditional devotional patterns. Their experiences are unusual. They, like traditional saints, live at the outer limits of human endeavour. Christians without boundaries. Where they live their lives, where they find their God, is often beyond us, in unfamiliar places. Their extremeness even may put them in touch with the divine. Most of us don't go there and know little or nothing of the experience, or of the toll it can take on the lives of these unusual people. Of course not all social reformers lead spotless personal lives. Pierre Toussaint apparently did. A Haitian slave who latterly lived in New York, he once refused to lead a peaceful protest march against slavery saying, "They do not know what they are doing. They have not seen blood flowing as I have." He was referring to his native Haiti.

In the South Africa of the Freedom Struggle, Toussaint would have been seen as lacking in courage, a sell-out or at least someone with a question mark over his true loyalties in the hour of need. African Americans might have called him an Uncle Tom, and Europeans perhaps a "moderate" black. Clearly he was not in the "saintly" socially involved league of Martin Luther King or Nelson Mandela. Recently, however, Pierre was made a venerable of the Church.

But, as I have pointed out earlier, traditional thinking might be changing.

Pope John Paul II canonised a Polish priest who was sent into exile after he took part in an uprising against the Russian Czar. "Of course that was a Polish priest", a cynic might point out. "Didn't the Pope favour his own?" Nevertheless there is hope that with the acceptance of the martyrdom of Oscar Romero of El Salvador the definition of holiness is expanding and becoming more inclusive. Coming from outside Europe, one of the first acts of Pope Francis was to unblock the archbishop's beatification process.

Chapter 15

The First Francis and Francis the First

Morena, nketse mosebeletsi oa khotso ea hao – Attributed to St Francis (English translation from SeSotho language: Lord, make me an instrument of your peace)

And what about our beloved Francis of Assisi? What made him a saint? Why is he the most remembered saint in the world? What is his attraction? Yes, I know he loved animals. We remember fondly this marvellous attribute of St Francis when every year clergy bless animals in hundreds of churches on the feast of the saint. But is it animals that Pope Francis from South America sees in St Francis from Europe? When he chose the name Francis, thousands of animal lovers probably expected that there would be pet cats and dogs, talking budgies and trained parrots abounding in the Vatican gardens and endless corridors in the not-too-distant future. Goldfish perhaps, even, in the Vatican fountains. The good times were here, thought pet shop owners around the world. Alas, it was not to be.

Francis of Assisi has long been associated with animals. Soon after his death people began to remark on how much he had liked animals when he was alive; of how he spoke to them so effortlessly. The birds listened to him too and even obeyed him, and a man-eating wolf accommodated him nicely in a forest near a place called

Gubbio. Unfortunately, some northern hemisphere cultures know of St Francis only because he loved animals. I don't think Francis made that impression during his lifetime. Pets were hardly tolerated that time. It's still the same among the poor today. Their strong sense of open-ended community seems to satisfy their immediate needs for companionship and unconditional love. And anyway a pet is one more mouth to feed. To believe that Francis lived for animals simply diminishes the man; it trivialises his message, given to us from Heaven. Yes, all the way from Heaven.

The Francis we are visiting is not a pious picture-card version of a saint bathed in heavenly light, who looks awkwardly out of place in the real world of you and me. There is more to it than that. Francis was never one-dimensional. He was rich in diversity and surprises and the unexpected. Not surprisingly, he is hardly remembered by Northern countries for his extensive travelling in the cause of peacemaking and reconciliation. After two World Wars, the United States, Europe and Japan know what peacemaking is all about. They have been there. Pockets of reconciliation, however, are still going on in these and other countries, even though many years have passed since the wars and conflicts ended. Francis travelled across the world in the pursuit of reconciliation. It wasn't easy, but he did it. Even at risk to life and limb. Peace-builders of the UN get killed even today in Bagdad, Kabul and Islamabad. Life can be raw, vicious and violent for those who wish to mediate peace. But more about that presently.

When he was sure of the call, Francis became a very driven young man. A very single-minded person. I guess all founders and saints are like that. Catherine of Sienna, Theresa of Lisieux, Clare and Francis of Assisi all told their incumbent Popes directly what they wanted – and they got it. I am repeating what I said before. They were all Olympic gold medallists in their own areas of expertise: spirituality.

Francis certainly won Olympic honours for spirituality, as we are seeing.

The life of St Francis throws up many striking features that are fascinating to recall and tease out. I want to stay with one of these for the moment; it might help my attempt to explain this very determined saint, a saint who some say has come to be loved and admired not only in America and Europe but also in Africa, Asia and South America. But is this true? Is St Francis really the world's most beloved saint? Beware of assumptions, dear readers. Francis can never be called the world's most well-known saint until the non-Western world can say they too own him.

Millions of people in our world are, however, mystified by Francis. For them animals are there for food, perhaps to guard the crops, or defend the family. Again, when Francis talks about the value of poverty – the *virtue* of poverty – the marginalised of this world, who do actually live in poverty, wonder can he be addressing them. People outside the West are shocked, too, when they hear that Francis abandoned his family. The ultimate sin against the community. And what was he leaving? Most religious readers of this have their story. How do you try to understand the route of Francis's calling? Grace builds on nature, some wise person said.

Francis's upbringing was beyond reproach. His were proud parents. They felt good about Francis. And he felt good about himself too. He had bright plans for the future. The neighbours were a little envious of the success of the Bernadones. They admired the boy, Francis, and the sensible way he was moving into his father's business. Just the way these things happen in well-adjusted families. A sense of continuity and family contentment.

A model family.

It's really hard to say when cracks began to appear and threaten the family unity. Mr Bernadone was heard shouting at times recently. In public he didn't let on that there were problems at home. Francis was being difficult, was the rumour. Something was coming over him. Pica, his mother, noticed it first. Mothers always notice things first. Francis looked tired, and behaved as if he were somehow bored. Perhaps more restless than bored. But more than that too.

Things were going from bad to worse. Was Francis simply browned off with the endless, and, for him, suffocating talk about business matters in the home? The constant chatter about bales of cloth, colours, textiles, fittings, prices, bargains, deliveries, materials, deadlines, price fixing, competition, deals and profits? Perhaps he found the discourse a little empty. Even draining and disillusioning. Perhaps the constant talk of clever bartering, thrifty saving, wise investing, favours for merchant pals, travelling dealers and dodgy salesmen left him cold. Did he find the daily flow of customers to the shop too much, perhaps even debilitating? Surely chatting up trendy celebrities who were seeking the best materials for their celebrations was stimulating? Was it not quietly satisfying to hear the friendly, rich and wealthy cheerfully making deals, and buying the best from his parents? Wasn't it fascinating and exciting for a young popular twenty-something-year-old to hear the top echelons of Assisi society, with keen eyes for quality, ordering fabrics from France for their annual town equestrian and archery festivals? The world of business and commerce was the only world he knew, and they were by and large decent people to deal with. He wondered why he could not be as excited as his father and mother about the business.

Francis wrestled with these anxieties and feelings for a long time. It wasn't a bad world that he was leaving.

His doubts and reservations deepened.

There was something that gnawed at his conscience, that didn't satisfy some yearning in him, that was drawing him away in another direction. Away from his family and his roots, away from his friends and relations. All very unsettling for those who knew and loved him. And probably for Francis too. Most people don't ever consider walking away from their families and cultures as an option in life. Most don't deliberately cut themselves off from their clans. Those who do are traditionally called drop-outs, vagrants or, in the 1960s, hippies. They leave home only for a period. They are still with us. Drop-outs. I once shared meals with them in a Christian ashram on the panoramic Bay of Bengal. They were mostly escaping from drugs in London or from personal or national issues like conscription in the South

African or Israeli armies. I remember one time celebrating Mass at the tomb of Christ in Jerusalem. A tall scraggy figure in a sari-like robe materialised out of nowhere and joined us as we were about to start. He was carrying a rosary as a sort of passport to the Holy Places. He was a white South African who had come to the Holy Land, he said, to avoid joining the apartheid army. Yes, this was happening at the time. But draft dodgers are, for the most part, temporary affairs. The dodger sooner or later returns to the society he left, settles down and has a family.

Earlier, Francis had actually joined his town army and went to war against a neighbouring city. He was captured and imprisoned. His family were devastated, especially his mother, Pica. Rumour had it that his father had ransomed him from prison in Perugia about a year later; more about this later. On one military campaign he did a U-turn, prompted by God. Another time he returned from a battle after a divine dream telling him to go home and wait for instructions. Perhaps he was an early conscientious objector, at a time when it was fashionable to win your army stripes and bring honour to the family name. A time when being a crusader was the ultimate accolade. Francis felt very much alone those days as he was nudged here and there by God. He came to know only gradually that the nudger was God, but how could he explain this to his parents and family? He was being called away.

Most people don't make a radical break with their own kith and kin. It is not normally called for today, unless you're sucked into a passing cult. I mean, how do you reject your own family values, your normal church routines, what you were taught by your teachers, and the life-giving company of your friends? But this is what happened to Francis, and probably with much personal pain. He even left a legacy of it for his followers, the Franciscans, lay and religious, of today. This is what interests us in the next chapter. People who are called to make radical and profound breaks with their past, sometimes disappointing if not shocking their parents and extended families.

So there were young things who were "radicalised" in the medieval world too!

Chapter 16

How Upper-class Francis Coped in the Culture of the Lowly Poor

> The Spirit of the Lord is upon me. He has anointed me to bring good news to the poor
> – *Luke 4:18*

In his autobiographical book, *Songs and Secrets* (Jacana, 2012) Barry Gilder quotes a letter his distraught mother wrote to him in 1976, after he had abandoned his privileged white South African background and gone to join the African National Congress resistance in the Angolan bush:

> You have crossed the Rubicon and closed all doors – to home, to your country, your family and your friends ... I cannot understand how your once gentle and sensitive soul could have succumbed to militant indoctrination ... You have done yourself a grave injustice by allying yourself with this kind of baseness ... In a way you have become dehumanised – you are not the same gentle, good-natured person you were – you have become ill at ease, morose, nervous, intransigent in thought. *Songs and Secrets, pp. 128–9*

Later in the book Gilder explains how he changed

radically when he broke with his family. He made an option for the poor and committed himself to solidarity with the oppressed and marginalised. In doing so he had to purge himself of the poison of racism. And during the process he discovered the power and value of sharing, and of community living. All noble Christian virtues – but in his case arrived at during the Cold War, under the tutelage of Marxist Soviet trainers and advisers supporting various liberation movements of the time.

> My intellectual political understanding had been shaped into a precise tool of experiential understanding and analysis. My middle-class individualism had been cleansed with the blood-flow of the collective. My soft body had been hardened by the calluses of work and soldiering. My guilt and hesitancy around people of darker hue had been washed away. My largely cerebral commitment to the struggle against apartheid had become deeply emotional, ingrained, interwoven with the past lives and newly shared experiences of the people I had lived with in the Angolan bush for over a year. (*Songs and Secrets*, p. 77)

Here, in a modern setting, we get something of the grieving and loss of a mother for a son taken from her by circumstances beyond her comprehension. We can imagine what she was going through, not only within her own family but also from the South African security apparatus and from "white" people in general. Mother and son later reconciled, and Barry Gilder is today a retired South African politician.

Pica Bernadone, Francis's mother, probably felt the same way about her own family's loss. Francis too made a very final break with his parents. You have only to think of the famous evening when Pietro Bernadone brought Francis's discarded clothes home after the incident with the bishop on the street and dropped them on the kitchen table. There was a horrible emptiness in the family that evening as they stared at the worn, lifeless garments of their son. A feeling even that he had been taken over by a cult or heretical group, of which there were a few in Assisi in those days. Pica sobbed as she tried to contain the anger of her husband who had been so publicly humiliated. There were moments she thought he was suicidal. I would like to believe, however, that later on the family were reconciled. Both of these sons were prepared to make great sacrifices for causes they believed in. One for an earthly cause, an earthly kingdom, the other for a kingdom of both here and the hereafter. Francis's gaze, to be sure, went beyond the here and now to the here and the beyond. His message and vision were to go global and were to endure for eight hundred years.

But let us not run ahead of ourselves. Let us continue to analyse, to accompany Francis, even to learn from him at close range as step by tentative step, he follows his unfolding dream. There was nothing his extended family could do to stop him. He was breaking all family ties. A final farewell on his terms. Unlike the past, when he had left for war, there were no send offs this time, no parties, no hugs, no speeches, no tears ... Well, maybe not "no tears". And so it happened. At a certain point in his young life Francis left his family for good, and asked to be admitted to the world of the poor.

And this is my second point. He was going somewhere. Not to his family, priest or bishop for advice. Not with his father to France on business. He was going to the poor. He was asking the poor to accept him. It happened over a period of time. God, he believed, told him to leave everything, even his culture; leave the lot, and join the poor jabbering masses. Before he resigned, Pope Benedict observed that globalisation creates "abundance for the few and misery for the many". Francis was now leaving the few and joining the many. Soon he was knocking at the door of the nobodies of society and asking to be accepted into their world. His family and friends wondered where his strange ideas came from. Perhaps he needed counselling? By today's standards he was eccentric. *Who was influencing him?* they whispered.

In the company of the poor, his new friends, Francis would have had to demonstrate his credentials, to prove his sincerity and to adjust to the conditioned minds of the underprivileged and the undernourished. Lest we forget: the poor have a way of thinking, a way of knowing, a way of solving problems and a way of getting things done. As a formerly privileged citizen of Assisi he would still have carried the marks of his affluent past and pampered upbringing. He was, after all, the son of a high-class family from Upper Assisi. No doubt he had problems dealing with a recurring sense of superiority when among his new company. But he was learning to listen, to hear new, unsteady voices and acknowledge new, disfigured faces.

Viewing his life, his Assisi, his parents, relations

and friends, and even the Church, from the vastly different perspective of the poor was a slow eye-opening revelation. It was an ongoing process of awkward adjusting to poverty, dependence and insecurity. His lack of control in his new austere surroundings, his vulnerability in the fragile world of the lower classes, was becoming the basis for a new spirituality, a new way of life: insecurity. Recently I experienced it at a supermarket checkout when I attempted to pay by parish debit card for the goods in the trolley before me. The assistant smiled sweetly as she told me my card was declined: dishonoured and useless. I dashed off to a neighbouring parish to borrow the balance needed. It was a lesson in insecurity, in dependence, in being vulnerable. This is the unsettling world Francis was moving into. When your electricity is suddenly turned off and you are plunged into the darkest darkness, groping for matches and candles, you get that sudden overwhelming feeling of disorientation. Francis was groping his way into this kind of world. Thousands of Americans, in both continents, who have been the victims of natural disasters know what the fragility of life is all about. They know what the experience does to you. Francis believed God was inviting him into this experience of vulnerability to free him for total dependence on the Divinity. Deliberately unhinging himself from past familiar props. In his new life as a wanderer for Christ, sweat, dust and dirt became his friends.

Many writers today urgently address us with "I hope you will find my life story inspiring" books. Critics feel there is now narcissism, a severe condition of self-absorption, with too many abuse and addiction memoirs in the bookshops. The affluent end of today's world, unlike Francis's medieval world, is fascinated by poverty. Especially its ravishes on human lives. Celebrities love to talk of their poverty-stricken childhoods. Look at the popularity of "misery memoirs" such as Frank McCourt's *Angela's Ashes* to appreciate that even today poverty in the Western world excites great attention and pity. People and the media love stories of harsh and deprived beginnings. Today rags to riches stories sell big time. Many have made a living out of them.

Nevertheless most people understandably want to escape poverty and know all about the "poverty eradication" programmes of their governments. Indeed poverty is evil. Poverty dehumanises rich and poor alike and can lead to envy, crime, hatred, racism, violence against those responsible for it, and often anger towards God. But Francis, always different, was going there, going towards poverty, rather than trying to escape it. For him it was a story of "riches to rags": rich man, poor man. Francis was embracing poverty because that's where God's dejected and exploited were to be found, and that's what the Gospel had told him in the little church that morning when he read the Bible at Matthew 10:9–10: "Do not carry any gold, silver or copper in your purses. Do not carry a traveller's bag, or an extra shirt, or sandals, or a walking stick." By now he was behaving in a very counter-cultural fashion. He was focusing on very unfashionable values: the values of the poor. He was highlighting the marginal culture of the sidelined. He found this liberating for himself too, as we mentioned earlier.

Let me bring in some clarifications at this stage about the role of the poor and poverty in the Christian life. After that we will continue with Francis and his story. As far back as 1976, Fr Albert Nolan, OP, the distinguished South African theologian, was writing:

> Jesus did not idealise poverty. On the contrary, his concern was to ensure that no one should be in want, and it was to this end that he fought possessiveness and encouraged people to be unconcerned about wealth and to share their material possessions. But this is only possible in a community. Jesus dared to hope for a 'kingdom' or world-wide community which would be so structured that there would be no poor and no rich. *Jesus Before Christianity* (David Philip, Cape Town, p. 53).

A namesake of St Francis, Cardinal Francis George of Chicago, explains how and why the poor and poverty speak to us today:

> Poor people are closer to the necessities and basics of life than many wealthy or middle-class people are. In this country, even our problems are luxuries that most of the world cannot afford. The poor cannot afford the illusion of personal independence. They therefore sometimes have a more immediate sense of dependence on God. At the time of the Second Vatican Council, Yves Congar and others spoke about a Church of the Poor.

Of course, no one should romanticise the poor; the poor are as sinful as anyone else. Catholics here have remembered what it was to be poor in the Great Depression and in the first generations of immigrants. Who wants to be poor? Involuntary poverty is certainly not an ideal in the sociological sense, but voluntary poverty is an evangelical ideal. The proclamation that the poor are the ones who are favoured in the Kingdom and that it is likely that the rich will go to hell is a sobering warning in the Gospels. Without conversion, we will collapse into the ways of those whom Jesus warned would lose eternal life.

There is nothing wrong with being wealthy or middle-class. It is the way of responsibility, the way of doing many generous and good things. The middle-class exists in order to set people free, including the poor; but if wealth is not dedicated to the wellbeing of the poor, and put to work in cooperation with them, then wealth becomes a road to condemnation. (*The Difference God Makes*. Crossroad Publishing, 2009, p. 183).

This teaching on the positive power of poverty is Bible-based, and Francis had found it and dusted it off.

What Francis was doing was something new in the Church for that time too. The sophisticated and erudite Pope Innocent III noted these developments and might have wondered if this movement, as Fr Hans Küng points out, could stem the rot in the Roman Curia: the nepotism, the favouritism granted to relatives, the acquisitiveness, the corruption and dubious financial dealings. No doubt Francis knew of these things, or at least those that were not covered up by the hierarchy. He operated out of another experience, thought of things differently – outside the box – heard dreams that puzzled him, and went into situations that puzzled others. It may well be difficult for academics and scholars to understand the mind of St Francis after he surrendered himself to the life and ways of the weak.

What do we know about the culture of the poor? The dynamics of grinding poverty among medieval peasants? Among the poor of today, living in barrios, favelas, under bridges, in squatter camps, in refugee camps, in ghettos, townships, informal settlements, shanty towns and forests? How do deprived communities discuss things, make plans and reach consensus? Living in the townships of South Africa for forty years has shown me, has taught me, a little of what it must have been like for St Francis. It helps me understand his journey from the centre of society to its margins. That Francis's journey should not be taken lightly. We dare not presume to know or to understand the motivations that guide a culture of deprivation, struggle, poverty and survival.

In writing this book I have discovered how difficult it is for writers on St Francis to know about the workings of the minds of the oppressed of the world. Or of the marginalised in our cities. How can writers get a feel for the daily rhythm, routine and rhyme of the values of the excluded? How do you react to someone, how do you cope with someone who has knowingly declassified himself – or herself – or reclassified himself, to use the racial terminology of the old South Africa? What startling behaviour for a man of his time, or any time. And it was all voluntary! Some thought he was a poverty-obsessed heretic like Peter Waldo protesting about the worldliness of the clergy.

In fact Francis was learning to listen to God through the living lost of society. That was new, perhaps even dangerous too, with a papacy at the height of its temporal power. Lowliness was not on the Church's agenda at that moment. Francis was learning the new values of the lowly. Values not known or experienced in his old life. Alien, indeed, to his old way of life. And still unknown in much of today's society. Francis was hearing and listening and learning that God was alive and well and active *outside* the walls, below the battlements, in the villages and among the lepers in the caves. Commentators now believe that the Reagan administration failed this listening challenge, this litmus test, when they sent in "advisers" to train the Contras in Nicaragua in the 1970s. They failed to crack the world of the poor. They took the wrong side, guided by smart agents who failed to decode the local signs of the times.

Nowadays, in countries where severe poverty or oppression exists, you will always find an alternative press, and community-based organisations listening and giving space to the voice and values of the otherwise voiceless. I worked and served in this climate for decades during the apartheid era in South Africa. This unique underground culture, tapped into, nourished and guided by the Christian churches, fuelled the downfall of apartheid in South Africa. I deal somewhat with this experience in my book *They're Burning the Churches* (Jacana, 2011). With that in mind it will always require great skill and sensitivity for a writer or journalist from America, Europe or Australia to capture confidently and comfortably the experiences of the outcasts of our time – never mind in the time of Francis.

It's humbling and thought-provoking.

There is, however, no reason to believe that Francis allowed himself to be consumed by the culture of the peasants. He didn't see himself as a missionary to them in the modern sense. It was rather that his growing mission included them. Indeed he needed the poor as much the poor needed him. The poor came to be Francis's vital link with God. Without this link he would have never been the Francis we know. His new calling, indeed, went far beyond their limited earth-bound aspirations.

The nudge of God, the pull of the Divine was upon Francis.

He was comfortable with any group, even the Charismatic Movement! He had no problem with spontaneous, heart-based prayer. One day, carried away in praising God, he asked a brother to write down what he was feeling:

> We should wish for nothing else and have no
> other desire; we should find no other pleasure
> or delight in anything except in our Creator,

Redeemer and Saviour; He alone is true God, who is perfect good, all good, every good, the true and supreme good. (*The Rule of Francis of Assisi*, 1221: 85)

Almost taken over by God, Francis was well into his conversion experience when he expressed these intense feelings about the nearness of God. But for the present, at the beginning of his journey, not only did he astonish, disturb and completely shock his peers in Assisi by "going native", but his journey into the poor of his day was to become a new sign of hope for the Church in the future. Of course very few understood this at the time.

For the sake of the present theme of Francis embracing the culture of the poor, I now invite the reader to visit a modern-day informal settlement with me. There we will find the serfs and peasants in their natural habitat. It is a fresh crisp Sunday morning and there is a flurry of activity at the ramshackle church. Puddles of muddy water channel the remains of yesterday's thunderstorm. The air is crisp and the African morning sun is so enticingly bright.

Chapter 17

Among the Serfs and Peasants in a Modern-day Shanty Town

> Brothers and Sisters, remember that God has called you in spite of the fact that few of you are wise according to human standards, or that few of you are powerful or members of important families ... God has chosen those whom the world considers fools, despised and unimportant in this world – *1 Corinthians 1: 26–29*

A few years ago, after the murder of my Franciscan colleague, Thabo Mokomele, I stood in one Sunday to celebrate the liturgy at his old parish of St Clare in Orange Farm, near Johannesburg in South Africa. St Clare's Church is a long, low shed, not much more than a shack, constructed by the parishioners themselves in the squatter settlement. It is Christmas time, in Orange Farm shanty town. Not that there is much to celebrate among the squatter people. No malls, no "shop till you drop" atmosphere, no mad rush or last minute shopping hysteria, no holly or mistletoe. No Christmas trees or gifts for the nieces and nephews. No Christmas cards exchanged. None of that otherworld fantasy. In fact, for those who live in places like this, almost the only reminder of Christmas is the odd carol you may catch on a community radio. And if the reception is good enough you're transported momentarily to the joys and infectious fever of the Christmas season growing up in Europe or America.

It's Sunday morning – church day – and everyone is wearing their simple but clean freshly-washed Sunday best. This is the day the community meet and share their lives in the way they were used to. Just like in Francis's time. The newly elected Parish Pastoral Council and Parish Finance Committee are busily going about their pre-Mass chores. The altar servers, as always, preparing – or perhaps, rather, constructing – the altar, fetching the water from a non-Catholic neighbour's shack, asking me for the wine I had, thankfully, remembered to bring, just in case, and whether I had brought breads to be consecrated. The Mass wine in times past and in other jurisdictions a cause for dissent among drinking and non-drinking servers! Thinking of problems with Mass wine reminds me of a story. In a remote rural parish the priest once told his parishioners there was no wine left for Mass in the following weeks. Concerned that their priest wouldn't be able to do a Cana-of-Galilee miracle the next Sunday, they came with a bottle of Red Heart rum, which they said would surely do because it sounded like the Sacred Heart of Jesus, the name of a well-known parish sodality. I'm not sure if the priest used it in the emergency!

A server takes my carrier bag and vanishes into the "church". From the car I spot a parishioner coming down the muddy, rain-washed dirt road carrying an old, frayed, newly washed Advent purple chasuble held up on a hanger to protect it from the wet mud. Arriving at the "church", he duly hangs it on a nail on one of the poles holding up the rickety structure.

Somebody calls me for confessions, so I'm shown into someone's shack bedroom and told the penitents are coming. I sit on a bed which takes up most of the room, and, one by one, the repentant sinners sit on the bed too, because there is no other space. The shack belongs to a Methodist family but they don't mind loaning it to the Romans for their Sunday service. Here the poor, the peasants and the plebs pour out their hearts and ask a forgiving God to look kindly on their daily struggles. And He does. Drunkenness, unforgiveness, abortion, revenge, affairs, jealousy, gangland capers ... and on and on, all with the mitigating circumstances of constant grinding poverty, lack of privacy, and AIDs eating away at the core of the community. I emerge after about twenty minutes, chastened and tired even before Mass has begun. In fact Mass should have begun fifteen minutes ago. Still people are arriving from all corners of the informal settlement. I don't know many of the people here but they seem to know me from other parishes I have served, which is nice. The township grapevine is enormous; everyone knows everyone – if you're living on top of one another you get to know your neighbours fast enough. I head for the church. Many greetings. Some old friends appear from the crowd.

I search for a sacristy. A sacristan shows me where to vest in a lonely little shed at the back of the church, about twice the size of an outdoor toilet cubicle. The servers are already there, in two rows, hands joined waiting to say the prayer and move off. From the "sacristy" we walk in procession to the makeshift church. God's shack. The newly assembled choir is singing – I'm not sure what – in anticipation. Entering the rickety building which heaves a little under a passing gust of wind, I spy the altar ahead, where an altar server is lighting some candles. I nearly trip on a protruding piece of rock near the entrance. The servers look around, some of them amused. Maybe I didn't suppress an expletive sufficiently. Even at this early hour of eight in the morning, the heat and smells of human sweat brush your face as you grow accustomed to the tiny, tinny structure. In his time this is where Francis and the brothers would have been found on a Sunday morning. Remember the simple rustic crib scene at Greccio.

Then I saw it just ahead. It was perched in front of the altar as if it was used to being there. As if it had been there for some time – perhaps weeks, I didn't know. Everyone was happy with that arrangement. I'm talking about the traditional Christmas crib. It's still two weeks to Christmas but the crib is in place and the figures are there for all to see. So Christ has arrived here two weeks before Christmas, I thought, with a touch of amusement! Francis would have been smiling. I don't think it worried anyone though. What are a few weeks between friends? Besides there was no liturgy committee yet in this new-born Catholic community. No liturgical panel beaters, no liturgical police in the pews to keep liturgical law and order. The peasants have more pressing matters to think about. But wait! This crib was different. The figures are not familiar. The composition is unusual. As I arrive at the altar I observe three mangy white dolls with blonde tousled hair, one of them without an arm. They seem to be like the famous Barbie dolls, their sell-by date long expired. They are standing awkwardly on newspaper in the crib.

Originally these Barbie dolls would have been very

sexy creatures. Not today. Their naked figures were quite unwashed – no doubt due to the regular township dust storms that whip up great clouds of fine dust which penetrates the most inaccessible of places in every home – and this long shack, the place of God, was no exception. Maybe the dolls had fallen into the mud on the way to the church and there was no water to wash them. They were accompanied by a yellow plastic duck, which I think was supposed to represent a cow. They had all been placed in a black plastic beer crate. That was the manger. One of the Barbie dolls was the baby Jesus; the armless one. I wondered did that represent the utter fragility of the Incarnation. This Christmas crib was – to my Western mind – really pathetic, lonesome and bizarre. But maybe these first-generation Christians didn't know the composition of a real crib. And, I reminded myself, it was the best these young Catholics could produce. They had tried, and that was great. I think Jesus loved it. He smiled too. This was a people who, like St Francis, wanted something visual to explain the extraordinary arrival of Jesus in our world. They had embraced the coming of the Christ in their own simple, and penniless, way. And they couldn't wait for Christmas to make it happen. (Talking of dolls and the liturgy—a fellow friar, Solly Mphela, told me while I was preparing this story, that he once witnessed, agonisingly, a parishioner in a remote out-station rushing to plant two big wind-up dancing dolls on the altar during the singing of the Gloria for Christmas morning. Nothing like enthusiasm; nothing like lay participation. Nothing like enhancing the joy of the Gloria. I suppose these dancing dolls could be called technical enhancements to the liturgy! Implementing Vatican II in a far corner of the earth, where soon there will be more Catholics than in the developed world.)

In the shed, Mass is underway. Reverence and rapt attention greet the readings. A young one still at school reads the early lessons followed by the choral singing of the psalm and response. Soon it is time to proclaim the Gospel. But there is a problem. There's a pool of water between me and the wobbly makeshift lectern at the other side of the altar, like a moat guarding the book of the Gospels. I noticed the servers when passing that way did a little, almost unnoticeable, unconscious jump. You couldn't say it was unseemly for it wasn't particularly pronounced and therefore wasn't distracting. Maybe I could do a hop, step and jump too, and land at the far side beside the open book? But that would be unseemly; it would take away from the dignity and sacredness of the moment. And would be unliturgical to boot. Something of the mystery of the occasion would be lost; the solemnity of proclamation would be compromised. But – my mind was racing – if there are liturgical dances then why not liturgical jumps? Encouraged by this idea, I decided to strike out for a momentary liturgy-without-borders, and hastened towards the book of the Gospels, bounding gently over the offending pool while preserving a solemn, deadpan, MC-totally-in-control face. I landed safely, but alas my heel hit the water, spraying the servers and the nearby faithful, who instinctively drew back, creating a human domino effect from this sudden minor tsunami. Slightly breathless, I steadied myself (while noting a twinge in my bad right knee) and read, or proclaimed or chatted the Gospel message, stopping here and there to explain something of significance to this community. South Africa is a Bible-reading country.

A seasoned missionary working in the hill country

of South Africa told me recently that many a time at this point in the hours-long African celebration, with a knowing nod to the servers, he would process solemnly from the altar with cross and candles (the servers insisted on this), down through the centre of the rural church, to the makeshift toilet outside, to satisfy the call of nature. Living close to nature and sensitive to its call is an accepted part of long liturgies in many parts of the world.

The Mass continues.

From outside, on a neighbourhood amplifier, soul singer Percy Sledge is now competing with our choir for attention. In fact his songs are the sound-background to all this morning's readings. I know, however, that the parishioners, used to constant human chatter in confined surroundings, were easily able to detect, discern and decipher the Word of God from the amplified musical surroundings. In informal settlements it's an easily-acquired ability. As was customary here, people would bring up their offerings to the altar at the offertory. But this time, as they did that, there was a funny incident. A mother holding her child approached in the slow-moving centre-aisle crush. The mother was struggling valiantly to extricate some coins buried under notes and scraps of paper in her purse. The child, spying the paper money sticking out of the top of the purse, grabbed them happily and deposited them in the covered collection box held by the lay assistant. The mother glared at the child very disapprovingly but could do nothing as she was nudged on by the people coming behind her. Actually the poor normally give more than the affluent for the upkeep of the church. But in this case the baby had outreached itself!

As I raise the host at the Consecration, the sound of Stevie Wonder singing *Superstition* bursts forth from a neighbouring shack. Not the ideal reception for the coming of the Creator. Again you absorb the situation. You'd better, for God is in the situation. But the birth at Bethlehem would have been much the same – animals don't go quiet just because a special baby is arriving. And the passion of the Christ happened in crowded, noisy market streets in Jerusalem, where busy shop owners barely paused while the divine procession passed by. Families had to be fed, they confided sagely; work didn't stop just because a "criminal" called Jesus of Nazareth was passing their premises on the way to the city execution site.

One thing is sure, all two hundred of this morning's congregation remembered every word of the Mass readings as serious nourishment for their journeys through life – their present life of survival in a cramped human settlement. And I knew that later they would be discussing these, and the homily, in their groups and families. It is now the time for the distribution of Holy Communion, and a slow shuffling queue is steadily approaching the altar. John Mokoena, crippled with knee arthritis, always insisted on kneeling for communion. This was a struggle for him nowadays, but generally he succeeded, though not without causing a stir among the communicants coming behind him. You don't have support like altar rails in a church made of tin sheets. Old John slowly lowers himself and, upon nearing the ground, falls forward on to his useless and life-battered knees. Mild consternation all round, especially from those coming directly behind. Distracted in their prayerful preparation for receiving the Body of Christ they patiently wait for the old man to complete his Sunday ritual on his knees. John is now ready to receive. Arching up his expectant mouth, his ancient tongue darting in and out, he grabs the Eucharist with his mouth, caressing my fingers with his saliva. But all is not over yet. Now he must return to an upright position. Now he must contemplate his ascent from this humble bodily posture. Hurriedly he blesses himself and in so doing accidentally hits my full ciborium with his hand. Six hosts scatter on to the mud floor between the moving feet of approaching parishioners.

Old man Mokoena, in his efforts to raise himself and be off, hasn't noticed. But the altar server beside me has. He doesn't rush off to find a purificator and dish of water in someone's house to wash the dry, muddy ground where the hosts had settled. He doesn't look at me quizzically wondering what to do next: as I bent down to retrieve the lost hosts from among the shuffling communicants' feet, he flashes past me, moving in the same direction. Before I can reach out my hand, he has grabbed the handful of hosts from the earthy ground and deposited them, dust and all, back into the ciborium. No consternation, no panic, no anxiety, no scruples, no wasting of time, no questions, and no sanitised rituals of cleansing. It was all helpfulness, instinct and common sense. The unexpected interruption had lasted only six seconds. Most people didn't even notice.

And the Mass continues.

By now we have been sacrificing in God's shed for nearly two hours, with a constant background of enthusiastic singing and celebration. Before the service ends, at least fifteen community matters are announced and discussed: last weeks collection, meetings, visitors welcomed, catechists reporting back, and so on. Announced because this is an oral society and news is transmitted mostly that way. Parish bulletins are unheard of. After the final prayer I wish everyone well for the coming birth of Jesus in appropriately blunt words or plain language: I wish them a hijack-free Christmas as well as a Christmas free from burglaries, robberies, mugging, abortion, adultery, violence, abuse of alcohol, loneliness, suicide ...

Afterwards people chatted outside for some time, many staying for their church group meetings.

Francis of Assisi and the brothers probably did the same and later slipped away.

Chapter 18

St Francis, War Veteran

> The atomic bomb in the hands of a Francis of Assisi would be less harmful than a pistol in the hands of a thug; what makes the bomb dangerous is not the energy it contains but the man who uses it – *Bishop Fulton Sheen*

Even the little I've told you so far about St Francis suggests that he was an out-and-out-extremist. Francis of Assisi was a medieval swank who appalled his contemporaries by voluntarily becoming a tramp. And the world has never got over this. So, many centuries later, people are still debating why he did this. And ever since then, his European biographers have been reining him in, trying to understand him, and perhaps reshape him a little.

Is there an unexpurgated, authentic, unmodified and official version of the story of Francis of Assisi? Why are people still asking about him, discovering him again after eight hundred years? Who is this thirteenth-century holy man that everyone wants to explain? Just when you thought you knew him, a new book appears – a new version of the saint, a new slant on the tramp. The saint everyone loves to love. The world media and many atheists, agnostics and non-believers have gone into overdrive about this particular saint. And the new Pope from the far end of the earth is not helping things. If fact he has stirred up international Francis fever. Yes, Francis of Assisi is still a curious enigma, an unexplained mystery, a kind of shooting star that brightened for a moment the world stage of our human history. What is the secret of his magnetic personality? Who was this frail-looking, unorthodox little man who outfoxed and outpaced Pope Innocent's medieval military machine, the Fifth Crusade? Would the Pope have approved Francis's rule of life if he had known that the little man from Assisi was going to pitch up at the coalface of the crusader war? I think it's reasonable, therefore, to ask: Will the real St Francis please stand up? Indeed, will he be permitted to stand up?

Let me explain a bit. I'll start in the middle.

Lovers of St Francis mostly don't remember his extensive ministry throughout medieval Italy in the cause of peace-building and reconciliation. I have mentioned this previously. An austere Ghandi-like figure, he was able to intervene quite imaginatively to bring peace where he found bloody discord, violence and tribal faction fighting. Or take the army, the military establishment of Assisi. These soldiers probably fought many wars during Francis's lifetime. And yes, Francis was involved in the fighting. He probably killed some of the enemy too, in close bloody encounters while at war. Northern hemisphere Christians won't like this image of their favourite, gentle, animal-loving saint. But we Franciscans make no apologies. And it gets worse. When Francis's biographers remember that startling escapade, his amazing peace pilgrimage to the north African city of Damietta, they're almost embarrassed! They're not sure what to say: Did he fail or not? They pass on quickly. That's why we know so little about it. So let us pause here in our narrative. Let us gaze a little more closely on that period of Francis's passionate, extraordinary life.

The following is a questioning, tentative (and not so light-hearted) reconstruction of aspects of the active life of the Bernadone boy (aka Francis of Assisi), from a non-European perspective. A perspective that will, I hope, enrich our knowledge of him, and expand what we already know. It also attempts to humanise Francis, to give him back to the people, and indeed to recall him as the all-including, global figure he was intended to be. Talking about global, I remember surreptitiously distributing 20,000 Francis bookmarks at the United Nations Climate Change Conference in Durban, South Africa in 2011. It was amazing how interested the non-European delegates were in these cards, especially the Chinese and those from Muslim countries. None were aware, not even the Europeans, who should have known better, that St Francis was the patron saint of the conference by virtue of being the patron saint of ecology. This was before Laudato Si, I might add. I think we need to take our saints out of their airtight boxes and let them be themselves.

Francis was still a fun-loving playboy when he joined the army. He learned what army life was about. He liked the feel and status of the uniform. His language was barracks language. His swagger was studied. The experience would help him when he joined the crusaders. It was like joining the marines for duty in Iraq or Afghanistan. Inter-city wars were common, and Francis was captured by soldiers from a neighbouring town and made a prisoner of war. The humiliation was devastating. The endless months in a medieval dungeon took their toll. While he was there, something happened to Francis. He began to notice that his thinking, his outlook was shifting to another place, another space. In spite of the dire prison conditions, he began to experience strange feelings, with a dawning, deeper peace that he had not been aware of before. Something was happening, he recalled later. It's true many saints have had profound mystical experiences in jail: Paul, John of Capistrano, Maximilian Kolbe to name a few. It was when he came out of jail that his close friends, the ex-combatants of Assisi, noticed first that something had changed. They said he was a little freaked out. A little removed from them in space and time. They wondered was he ill? Was it depression?

Francis was about to become a dropout. The greatest dropout and the loudest walkout in history.

Chapter 19

Was Francis Mad?
Or Just a Pained Dropout?

Sometimes ... he did curious things ... At times he picked up a stick from the ground and, raising it to his left arm and taking another in his right hand, he made as if to play the violin – From Brother Leo's memories of St Francis

A savage madman who spoke to animals, gave religious instructions to a wolf and built himself a wife out of snow – Voltaire (1694–1778)

Francis began to act strangely, to do things differently. Which caused more talk. His closest friends were baffled. Some drifted away. There was no point they said. The bawdy humour had diminished. The girls were fading from his hitherto clear line of vision. He no longer pinched wenches, banged tankards and called for more ale. Peer influence was becoming less and less a factor in his life. At home Francis was rapidly losing interest in carrying on his father's business. He didn't have the aptitude, or at least chose not to show it if he had it. He was less and less motivated by profit, hard work, success and achievement – the ingredients that drove the family textile business. One day he was caught giving away bales of imported linen from the family shop. His father,

Pietro, went berserk – justifiably.

By now his parents were clashing with him, and among themselves, over his mood changes. It was more than hormones. Like many a young person he left home, but it was for more than a "gap" year. He left for good. There was something very final about it. His parents were gobsmacked. With his new-born self-awareness, Francis was fast outgrowing his parents' spirituality – a quiet but startling realisation in any person's life. It was very disconcerting for all concerned, the aunts and uncles too. For his mother and father there was private grieving, and indeed loss, in their relations with their son. For Francis, it was surely a lonely, singular and sad breaking of ties with his beloved parents. He felt more on his own than ever before. Simultaneously, he felt strongly a need for new space, a new independence in his life. The lure of something beyond the family was becoming more insistent, more definite and demanding. This reached crisis level one famous day when Francis publicly, before bishop and citizens, stripped naked and then returned the clothes from his back to his uncomprehending father. His poor father must have been completely crushed by this public spectacle. At that moment, in this mad event, he knew he had lost his son and indeed that his son had lost himself. He felt helpless, damaged, let down and betrayed. He had hoped that the bishop would have knocked some sense into his son's stupid head.

Mr Bernadone was a respected member of Assisi's business community. This we know. The business world within the feudal social system had made him fairly well off. A hardworking husband and father, by all accounts he loved his family. It was the only thing he understood, the only life he knew. He had done everything for his family, giving them a comfortable life and a prosperous future in the import-export business. If he were alive today he would be serving on his Parish Pastoral Council, or perhaps better still as a businessman and member of your local Parish Finance Committee. And now this. An errant bloody fool of a son, who implicitly questions the very foundations of his father's business life is any man's nightmare. The bottom was slowly falling out of his life. Why had this happened? Where had he gone wrong, he asked himself again and again. Pica, his wife, could not console him. Often at night during those winter months when he was not away on business in France, he would just sit there slouched before the family fire, staring into the dying embers.

Chapter 20

"Go Repair my House" the Crucifix said to Him

And Satan trembles when he sees
The weakest saint upon his knees – *William
Cowper (1731–1800)*

Francis had drifted away by now. One day news filtered
back to the family, or it was rumoured, that Francis had
had a peculiar experience before a cross in an abandoned
church called San Damiano. Kneeling to pray before the
main altar that morning, he heard a voice coming from
the crucifix say three times, "Francis, go and repair my
house which, as you see, is falling completely into ruin."
Probably what this message meant didn't dawn on him
immediately. But he sensed a strange energy was
present. A strangely peaceful energy. It was addressing
some core area somewhere inside him. Moments of
consternation, of ecstasy, of indescribable upliftment
seemed to follow. And after that, he remembered later,
profound feelings of consolation and reassurance that he
was doing the right thing. And then quiet; calm; birds
twittering in the background emphasising the silence. He
just sat there and waited, and wondered what was
happening. Divine guidance was happening before his
eyes in this little abandoned medieval church on the
plains. Was this the cost of leaving your family for a new
life? he thought. He looked around but there was no one
in the abandoned church. A dog barked in the distance.
A dove cooed from a rotting rafter.

Again he looked up at the icon crucifix over the altar, and slowly he began to talk to it, to pray. As he talked, he realised that he was being addressed, being called and given a mission by God. A vocation. Things were still coming into focus though. His journey was intensifying. Later, walking alone up the hill to Assisi he realised that this experience had further confirmed his recent decisions. It helped him to see a way forward. It was one of many life-wrenching experiences he'd had lately; a sort of divine approval of his recent wanderings.

And, of course, there was Francis's life-changing meeting with the leper while he was out riding at around that time. That really blew his mind, his whole being. He had embraced a leper, an untouchable. It had happened while they were alone in an open field, on a pathway just below the town of his birth. They had to be alone because outcast lepers were just that: cast out. In 1206 they were never allowed anywhere near a residential area. For Francis, embracing a leper was life-splitting, an emotional lightning bolt, a spiritual tsunami – verily the hand of God. Francis was still unbundling himself. His past and present values were colliding dangerously. He was trying to sort out new priorities recently received from only-God-knew-where. In fact it was a process, a series of events – spiritual events and encounters – that he submitted to that was changing him. In quaint mountainous villages like La Foresta, Greccio, Poggio Bustone, La Verna, Fonte Colombo, in these rural towns and villages Francis was to become a sort of holy celebrity.

Hovering in the background, perhaps even an added anxiety for Francis, was the beautiful, determined and unorthodox Clare, bent on becoming part of Francis's growing movement. No wilting lily was she: one time she repelled attacking Muslim mercenaries by raising a monstrance with the Blessed Sacrament over them. Until her dying day she kept insisting that the Pope approve her radically new rule for religious women. The Pope, defeated, gave in while she was on her death bed. An early victory for religious feminism! The Poor Clares, like the Dominicans who inspired the great Catherine of Siena, are still giving life to the world after eight hundred years. More about this lady later.

Something bigger than Francis was happening. Something bigger than most people could cope with. God had told him to leave everything. To break with the way of life he had been born into. He was walking away from the family values he had grown up with. He had made the break, which as we know had been no easy task. Next, God had told him to seek after the poor and their outlook. This had been much more difficult. It was so public. The abuse he received, the misunderstandings, the embarrassment to the family. All this activity, all this pressure on Francis, all this muffled calling to a new way of living was really preparing the world for a revolutionary return to the basics of Christianity. God was using Francis as a new pointer, a new herald to Christ's ground-breaking attitude to the poor, possessions, and poverty. In all this God hadn't told him what movement to join or where to go, apart from repairing a little church on the plain below Assisi. Should he join the long established Trappists or Benedictines in search of solitude? (For the local bishop, and indeed for the Pope of the day, the imperious Lothario of Segni, Innocent III, this would have been a nice neat solution for the case before them.)

By now God had radicalised Francis. He had become a misfit, most people agreed, and wanted to live a life of misery. Was he mad? the good people of Assisi asked. Was he stark raving mad? In the quietness of his heart he was discovering in his new friends, the poor, the different faces of Christ, and beginning to see events in his own life from *their* perspective. Such an attitude was quite unusual for that time. For any time, really. In the language of today, Francis was going along the path of a sort of liberation theology before its time. Liberation theologians today would call it "solidarity with the poor". Pope Benedict, eight hundred years later, readily agreed when he told us in Brazil a few years back that the "preferential option for the poor is implicit in Christological faith".

But no saints had done it that way before. The clergy were worried. This was innovation where it was not welcome. How many saints or founders of orders or congregations have gone through hell, utter nightmares, when they dared suggest renewal within their own congregations? Never mind coping with followers who were materialising out of nowhere. What he was willing to do shows the amazing vision of Francis. This was a new way to come to God. He was searching for the "poor and weak, who are our teachers" (in the words of Pope Gregory the Great). So not only was he withdrawing from the driving values of his family, culture and society, he was being fatally attracted to the other side, outside the walls, the unimportant and forgotten, the invisible ones. It was there, among them, he was coming to believe, that Christ was embedded and accessible. Yes, that was it, accessible.

Christian missionaries in South America, Africa and Asia can relate to that. It happens. Priests, religious and lay volunteers will know what I'm talking about. The encounter with the leper had been crucial to Francis's changing identity. It was frightening for his family. Another frightening cultural turnabout.

Chapter 21

Francis Confronts the Politicians and the American Gun Lobby

> When a society – whether local, national or global – is willing to leave part of itself on the fringes, no political programmes or resources spent on law enforcement or surveillance systems can indefinitely guarantee tranquillity – *Pope Francis, The Joy of the Gospel: 58*

In his discernment, Francis was beginning to see the society that he was a part of as sinful in many ways. Instinctively he did a See, Judge and Act social analysis (remember the Young Christian Workers?), and concluded that something was rotten in Assisi – the Assisi that he had militarily so vigorously defended. And to think that he had at different times defended that society. He cringed at the thought. He was beginning to feel uncomfortable, a stranger, in his place in feudal society. The system was, yes, ungodly. It dawned on him that these uncaring, selfish structures (since then we've seen them in communism, nazism, apartheid and even in capitalism) were inflicting terrible suffering on the peasants and the poor. Tortured by his new consciousness, Francis finally had to walk away. As we have seen he turned his back on his society.

As I write these lines I'm suddenly aware of something that happened only this very morning. I drove some African township youth to our Franciscan postulancy near Johannesburg to begin their life as Franciscans. I noticed that they'd brought a vast amount of luggage with them. Cases, bags and bundles. I didn't get the feeling they were radically turning their backs on their society. Certainly Francis was – on everything his extended family and friends stood for, and had died for in the interminable wars of the time. Would Francis have called the feudal system a sinful society whose sinful structures were created by individual sinners? As in the cases of communism, nazism or apartheid?

Time passed. Francis the living saint was emerging.

One day, outrageously to many, Francis publicly provoked city politicians by declaring at his treasonous best that he was "a servant only of God, and no longer owe[d] allegiance to civil authorities". Today there are still plenty of countries who imprison people who say things like that. Perhaps this was Francis's way of standing up against a worsening political situation. He was saying that enough was enough. He felt that leaders had replaced genuine piety and integrity with corruption, greed and support for sinful, evil structures that abused people. Another time, in a written memorandum, Francis chided political leaders for their waywardness, their giving politics a bad name. And they didn't like it one bit. They were disgusted and embarrassed at his daring. They told him to keep out of politics! Politicians hate clerics voicing their opinions about politicians and politics, especially corrupt politicians and corrupt politics. Many erstwhile friends thought Francis had finally lost it. They said so.

These were violent times. Like Argentina in the seventies and South Africa in the eighties. It becomes increasingly clear to me that Francis would have been comfortable with the Christian activists of our time who engage in peaceful civil disobedience. Given the number of letters he wrote to a wide spectrum of people, we can be certain that he was a man who wanted to see results in his lifetime. His ministry of letters, his social engagement showed that. And where did the Church stand? In this case the hierarchical Church. What was the position of the Church, the place of the Church, in this dysfunctional society? What witness, if any, did the bishops and priests give? What was their role and service? Pope Benedict, speaking of St Francis in February 2010, offered a clear answer: "The ruinous state of that church was a symbol of the dramatic, disturbing situation of the entire Church of that age, with its superficial faith that did not form and transform people's lives, and with a clergy that was not zealous." The Church was "decomposing from within", he said. Now think of the recent explosion of child abuse scandals rocking that same Church today.

Did Francis abandon this "decomposing" Church like so many in his day – and so many today – when its human side showed signs of failure? Not Francis. He was made of something else. He had already submitted himself to Jesus as his Lord and Saviour. Nothing could budge that conviction. Not even a corrupt clergy. But wait. Didn't he admonish his followers to respect even rotten priests, on account of their priesthood and their ministry of the Eucharist? Francis's spirituality enabled him, and other saint reformers, to discern the presence of Christ in the sometimes-sinful hands of the institution. Today we pray for those brothers and sisters who, scandalised, have walked away from the Body of Christ because of the abuse scandals. In fact scandal and corruption has always happened in the church starting even with the conflicting faults of the apostles Peter, Mathew and Judas. Indeed it was Mathews' Gospel (13:30) which taught that in the end times God would separate the weeds from the wheat, the good from the bad. In Francis's time thousands abandoned the Church, deeply hurt by what they saw happening. They started their own movements, or joined others. The more well-known sects were the Albigensians (Cathars), the Waldensians and the Humiliati.

Those who walk away like the above have their critics too. They, lay or cleric, are accused of claiming a special line to God even if unsaid, and often pandering to the public their own populist "truth" centered on themselves like sometimes deluded visionaries, angry celebrities or fixated impractical idealists. Francis, lately watchful of these temptations, was too close to God to abandon his church, a church of saints and maddening sinners. We live in the hope that God will continue to intervene, purge and purify his Church every time it needs it, whether by raising up people like Francis, Clare and Dominic or sending the media to expose the accumulating evil often bubbling below the surface.

Before I leave this chapter I must mention something else. Where Francis raises issues with modern counterparts: disarmament.

Let me explain.

There are people, many of them non-Americans, who firmly believe that America jumps into troubled waters in our world without due reflection. They cite recent wars around the globe. Guns and bombs, they claim, are seen as America's solutions for most problems. Guns for self defence and getting even and bombs for solving international political problems. But wait. People did the same in the time of Francis and he would be the first to tell you that. Indeed, there was a period in his life when the sword and dagger were extensions of himself and he savoured it self-consciously whenever he sauntered into the best ale houses in Assisi. It was the time he lived by the sword and nearly died by it too. The powerful super "patriotic" gun lobby in the United States is of the same mind of the early Francis. A tad like some South African super whites conspicuously brandishing guns during the apartheid era.

Enter the "Wild West". Yes, the Wild West, the raw rough frontiers of America where life was cheap and violence natural. America's gun lobby reminds us, without intending to, that the West has not yet been won. They somehow tell us that the crusty pioneers of the plains are still with us and that only fools and dummies would swagger around a frontier town unarmed like anxious bankers, hardened saloon owners and the "Godly" Elmer Gantrys of old.

Today guns are so easily available a high noon skirmish at Tombstone can break out at any moment in any school, at any church, on the streets of the southern states, or in cinemas and other places where crowds gather. Not to mention the shooting of four monks killing two, by an old man wielding and assault rifle at Conception Abbey, Northwest Missouri in July 2002. On cinematic evidence Hollywood is still shooting down aggressive aliens, shadowy spectres in paranormals and weird sci-fi monsters clanging flatfooted over First World metropolises. The culture of bloody death is still alive and well.

To appeal to the gun lobby in America, to reduce their mortal dependence on lethal weapons is like asking Wild Bill Hickok or Billy the Kid to leave their Winchesters and six-shooters at the entrance of Deadwood in South Dakota in 1823. It could not be done. A sheriff could never enforce it. Not even that unlikely multicultural couple the Lone Ranger and Tonto could do it. The tinsel screen has always demonstrated to us, to the planet at large, that life's problems are ultimately solved by a televised war or a "Gunfight at the O.K. Corral". Or in the language of today when the hand of our hero in New York is caught on close up camera slipping into an office drawer to retrieve a little used 9mm Parabellum. As he readies the breach for action his determined face says it all. Clint Eastwoodesque. We know the end is nigh!

This free lesson in violent conflict resolution impresses and inspires the criminals in the world for the next thirty years as the movie makes its rounds to every city, town and village on earth. Criminals living on the poor peripheries of the world love the sound of American gunfire solving everyday problems. According to one recent survey, the average American child has observed 18,000 killings[7] before graduating high school. And is it true that over 12,000 people died in gun violence in the USA in 2015? In Francis's time most carried their weapons for self defence. It was part of their dress. And the sword and dagger lobby were happy with that arrangement. It was never questioned. I mean popes and clergy carried arms to war too. They had to defend the church and its lands and properties from marauding warriors, roaming Saracens, paid mercenaries, local warlords and foreign armies. It was taken for granted.

What a shock then when Francis, out of the blue, told his followers not to carry arms. Period.

---

[7] Brian McClinton () *Humanist Ireland* p.7

Chapter 22

The Street Theology of Francis

My God, give me happiness – not Nietsche's tragic and ferocious happiness, which I do admire, but St Francis happiness: a radiating happiness worthy of adoration –
André Gide

Why should they continue to wear arms? They had nothing to defend, Francis told his followers. Stark raving mad was the verdict of his contemporaries and followers many of whom were proud of their military pasts. Were you to lay down your arms when you should be defending the Papal States and joining the Pope's Crusade? His father, it was reported, went into a rage once again. How could he do business without proper cover? Without defensive weapons. But Francis was talking to the early brothers. And he was addressing another way of life. Undermining family and society values. And nailing them into a coffin by telling the brothers in no uncertain terms not even to carry coins. He was deconstructing "the artificial levers of power and privilege" in society and in the church. This was the real St Francis; the quietly subversive St Francis. The undomesticated St Francis. The Francis freeing himself to be led by the imaginations of the Holy Spirit. To do this, to create a new society he really had to walk away lovingly from family and friends. Otherwise they would have undermined his every move and thought, his every creative idea or spiritual insight.

In some ways this is the beginnings of religious life even today.

From his unlettered writings there is no doubt that the son of prosperous Assisi's best known businessman became obsessed with the personality and life of Christ. All serious students of Francis of Assisi agree that somehow he succeeded in penetrating the mind of Christ better than most. This Francis-on-Christ phenomenon, distilled through his larger than life personality and through his experience of conflict and violence, has fascinated the world for eight hundred years.

This raises an interesting point.

What is the impact of violent times on the creative spirit of a person? Distinguished Jesuit palaeontologist, Pierre Teilhard de Chardin, who experienced a "baptism into reality" as a stretcher-bearer in the frontlines of World War I, recalled: "For my own part I can say that without the war there would be a world of feelings that I would never otherwise have known or suspected."[8] De Chardin, therefore, like Francis, found a type of illumination in the turmoil and tumult of war, or, as he described it, "a light which danger enkindles within". Francis, like Clare, had survived life-threatening situations. This would have altered and deepened his outlook, his vision and his understanding of reality. It

---

[8] Pierre Teilhard de Chardin (1965) *The Making of a Mind: Letters from a Soldier-priest 1914–1919*. Harper & Row.

also would have made him more fearless, more assured, more confident and willing to encounter risk and face a radical future in the service of God and Church.

Today, apart from the two World Wars, the social "danger" that might trigger spiritual illumination is found mostly in the global south. The life-threatening experiences of political conflict of many missionaries living in the South will confirm it. They have been there and back. They have had an "experience" of God, a mystical experience, the richness of which has gone mostly unrecognised and unacknowledged by academic theologians. Through these mind-jogging, life-changing encounters many missionaries have been challenged to roll back the parameters of received spirituality, pastoral theology and pastoral practice. The theology – or lack of it – behind seismic human struggles such as colonialism, apartheid or the genocide of Rwanda must not be ignored by mainline theologians.

No informed biblical or liturgical scholar would dare ignore the international legacy of South Africa's Kairos Document of the 1980s. This document, which successfully undermined the established Calvinist theology of apartheid, is a reflection on the biblical understanding of oppression. During the eighties in South Africa it fuelled inter-church solidarity, resistance and the creation of history-making liturgies leading, ultimately, to the downfall of apartheid. These particular sources of spiritual and theological enrichment have not yet been captured and interrogated in the classrooms of religious and clerical formation. Crisis ministry, the practical application of the principles of Kairos theology, is not for the faint-hearted. Street theology, the faith reflections of people on the streets and in their homes, in their actual nitty-gritty everyday situations, can change lives and renew the world as we know it. Pope Francis comes from this type of developing-world background, and through his exhortation *The Joy of the Gospel* explains his missionary outlook to a surprised Western world.

I raise the above points for a particular reason. To broaden our understanding, as I see it, of the thirteenth-century man Francis. I come to these impressions, these insights of Francis, from my own experiences of conflict and ongoing rolling revolution over a period of forty years in South Africa. The traditional European Franciscan teaching of the born-again Francis is to demonstrate always his loyalty to the Church and its teachings. Writers and lecturers talk of his great reverence and love for the Eucharist, for prayer, poverty, obedience, for Mary, the Trinity, the Sacraments, and the role of the Cross – and of how these can affect our own spirituality. And this is absolutely correct, despite the fact that some scholars have tried to detach Francis from the Church and its teachings.

But the real Francis was more than his teachings. Many lovers of Francis are tempted to split his personality, to redefine him, to make him conform to a more static spirituality. His deepening understanding of the faith was not, however, a static understanding. He couldn't believe that faith stood still. It had to lead somewhere. It had to be an evangelising faith – an evangelising faith that penetrated deeply into the broken Body of Christ. An evangelising faith that questioned the usually unquestioned assumptions proclaimed by the clerical and secular fathers of his time.

So Francis was more than his teachings. But if we concentrate only on his loyalty to the Church, we can easily overlook the fact that many of his activities were a direct reaction to Church and State arrogance, violence, corruption and evil. Today, at this moment, there are new types of arrogance, violence, corruption and evil in our world and in our Church that challenges the lovers of St Francis to imagine new options, to contemplate new solutions, and to explore new choices.

Chapter 23

With Francis in a Liturgy of the People, by the People

Without the worship of the heart liturgical
prayer becomes a matter of formal routine –
Dom Aelred Graham, OSB

Francis loved the liturgy. For him it was an experience of
thanking, praising, hearing and facing God. It affected
him. It stirred him. It moved him. It inspired him to
imagine the world he was coming from as a world
transformed into God's likeness. It was as simple and
natural as that. The main church in Assisi, the cathedral,
was the site where great feast days and solemnities were
celebrated. Francis and a few of his first followers always
stood near the back of the cathedral; the rich, the famous
and the powerful would be found in the reserved spaces
at the front. These were the rich, the famous and the
powerful he was to chastise publicly at one stage – as we
saw earlier.

But that's only an aside. Let's come back to the
feast day celebrations in the Cathedral of Assisi. Was it
San Rufino? The sanctuary was always full of moving,
mostly portly figures caught in glorious shafts of morning
light from lofty windows. Francis's imaginative mind
couldn't help thinking of stuffed, overdressed dolls as the
senior clergy shuffled around the incense-filled Holy of
Holies, proudly dressed to kill in elaborate vestments,
looking stern and feeling desperately important. For

Francis and his simple followers there was an unreachable air about these lavish liturgies. The ceremonies were oh so cerebral, so cold, so clerical, so theatrical, so perfect in execution, so predictable and so worldly. It was so often Show Time. The first friars, like any would-be reformers, felt left out, excluded and alienated.

One Sunday after Mass Francis got an idea. It was early December; there was still time. He explained his plan to the brothers. He would create his own ceremonies, his own liturgy for Christmas. He was a person who instinctively liked tangible, dramatic action. What if he dramatised Christmas? Kept alive its memory in a different way? And yes, it could be enacted right here with the Christmas Eucharist. And so it came to pass. Francis and his closest followers did a sort of morality play for those who were interested. A people's liturgy in a very cold mountain cave, appropriately sheltering domestic animals. They kept it simple; only the brothers and the peasants from Greccio were present. The storyline was Christ coming to our earth, becoming a citizen, and making us all brothers and sisters. Francis couldn't get over this mystery, this fabulous gesture of God. Pondering it brought him out in goose bumps!

Francis was probably a deacon, for he sang the Gospel that Holy Night with great intensity and emotion, with one of the brothers unsteadily holding up the heavy book of readings. Perhaps Bro Leo was the celebrant. It was surely a rare community experience. A very moving celebration of the Incarnation. An intensely moving moment. And to add divine favour to the occasion, one of the simple faithful saw a baby appearing mystically in the manger, to be awakened and embraced by Francis! There were tears on many a grubby, rustic candle-lit cheek that night! Tears of recognition, tears of joy, tears of longing, tears of rapture. Even the priest who celebrated the Mass for them was overcome with joy. For the small crowd of simple people it was a night they always remembered. A spiritual experience for the poor. And they told their friends afterwards. And that's how the crib we see in our churches each Christmas came into being; it was another first for St Francis.

One of my lecturers at All Hallows College in Dublin described liturgy as "play", as "totally useless but profoundly meaningful". I have known many liturgies that would fit that description. I mean there is no purpose in going out to a restaurant for a meal unless for a convivial get-together, and a chat about what's going on in our various worlds. Isn't liturgy supposed to be about our lives? About what's going on in our lives? I think Francis would have said yes to that. A definite yes. Liturgy is celebrating our lives. The Greccio Christmas was that for St Francis. And Africa, with its gift of natural spontaneous celebration, would have understood and enjoyed Greccio that night.

Chapter 24

Francis and Extreme Ministry

The Samaritan woman became a missionary immediately after speaking with Jesus and many Samaritans come to believe in him 'because of the woman's testimony' (John 4:39) – *Pope Francis: The Joy of the Gospel, 120*

As Francis fell increasingly under the spell of Jesus, he was led to become a willing instrument in social peacemaking. "The Lord give you peace," this ex-army man greeted all and sundry with – pointedly, for there was little tribal harmony in his medieval world. Indeed it was a period of inter-city butchery. "Kill, kill, kill!" was the war cry often heard across the rich vineyards and valleys.

Now Francis begins a new ministry. There were no emails, no mobile phones, no Twitter or Facebook in those days. No "social networking" was in sight. The first brothers were constantly telling him about the violence in their home towns and villages. Sometimes their families were involved. At any rate he knew that all was not well in the Italy of those days. War, violence and faction fighting was rife, was everyday stuff. He prayed about it, thought over it, and felt he had to do something. He decided to act, to speak up and to explore where he could help. He became a counter-sign to the numerous ongoing inter-city wars. He openly rejected his former military way of solving problems. No need to call in the soldiers. Swords and daggers represented a lifestyle he was leaving behind. "Go and preach peace to all", he told his surprised followers one rainy morning after they'd all had a bite to eat. He set out on his first journey of peace.

In a forested hill area north of his birthplace Francis used food to make peace where a notorious gang had been terrorising the local township people of San Sepulcro. He brought reconciliation to another town called Arezzo, not far from Florence, that was being devastated by constant bitter squabbling among brutal warlords, as they still do in Afghanistan. He sent Brother Sylvester to Arezzo and told him to sing a hymn at the city gates. Incredibly, it brought peace. Yes, Francis was different. Brother Sylvester knew this because Francis had already done some weird things for peace. (It reminds me of the time that Bono, of U2 fame, brought political opponents on to the stage during a Belfast pop concert.)

In Bologna, in the north of Italy, Francis's apparent humility and hippie-like disinterest in creature comforts inspired peace talks between citizens who had until then hated one another. In Siena, future home of that magnificent political peacemaker, St Catherine, Francis brought peace by persuasion to two warring factions bent on annihilating one another – much as there was in the former Yugoslavia, or is in present-day Iraq. He used his own home-grown liturgies, incorporating the parties involved, to achieve peace and reconciliation in the most unlikely situations.

Why did Francis appear to go further, to minister beyond the boundaries and parameters of local institutions, municipalities, customs, parishes, churches and even dioceses, and yet retain the friendship and protection of the ecclesiastical authorities? How did he get away with it? He knowingly subverted the social and political conventions of his day by forbidding his lay followers to carry weapons. This at a time when it was normal for everyone to carry knives, cutlasses, daggers or swords to protect themselves from ever-present death squads, thugs and highway robbers. He was like that. Is like that. You just don't know what he's going to do next.

Another peace story. In the town of Assisi the bishop couldn't stand the mayor and the mayor had a singular dislike of the bishop. It was the talk of the taverns. At public functions the two leaders studiously ignored one another; it was very noticeable. They never sent invitations to each other either. Event managers knew not to seat them anywhere near each other. Sometimes the mayor didn't even turn up if he knew the bishop had been invited. For months it went on like this. Finally the bishop, in a fit of spiteful anger (he was known for his short temper) excommunicated the mayor. The mayor, returning from Foligno that morning, was dumbstruck when he read the letter of excommunication. "Stronzo!" he was heard muttering as he plopped into his black velvet chair of office. His Worship, the mayor, was quick to retaliate. He forbade citizens from doing business with the bishop. Tit for tat. People began to take sides. Things were getting out of hand. Into this situation stepped Francis Bernadone, previously the city oddball but more recently seen as someone with unusual insights into matters of the human spirit. No longer the butt of people's jokes, but rather a respected, saintly person. A saintly person who got things done, who was often proactive in his ministry; who worried about the state of the Church as he saw it in Assisi.

Medieval rows were very public affairs. As in today's townships and barrios, the houses were on top of one another. All one big chat house. Word got around like lightning. In that context you had the mayor-and-bishop feud. It had been going on for some time. It was bad for city morale; it was a scandal in the town. Again he prayed about it and decided to do something. To take the initiative. He believed intervention was now called for. Uninvited intervention. (One of Francis's great pastoral contributions to evangelisation was his uninvited, timely interventions.) The clergy had tried and failed. Francis hadn't studied conflict resolution methods. In his former career you solved problems with the sword, the lance and the dagger. Young, able and arrogant, he had been trained for war, not peace. He had learned to take problems head on. He didn't, therefore, shy away from conflict situations. He faced them, eyeball to eyeball. He was almost attracted to them, indeed. Look elsewhere in this book for proof.

Some, including the brothers, said it was none of his business being involved in these political matters. They felt Francis should be paying more attention to establishing a stable religious life for the new recruits who were flocking to him. How could they have known that he was inventing a new type of religious life – starting a new type of religious group – and that they were its first members? But young Bernadone thought peace-building *was* his business. Prophets think differently. Francis was a novice prophet whose day had come. Have you ever noticed how founders of new orders and congregations in areas of evangelisation are so sure of themselves? Perhaps it's a God-given stubbornness, necessary for what God wants them to do. Something to confound the naysayers and the objectors!

One day an ailing Francis called the bishop and the mayor to a meeting. He would be a mediator, he said. But alas, just then Francis had a turn for the worse. In fact he was dying. Yes, this story is from late in his life. He couldn't come in person, so he called the bishop and mayor together near the bishop's palace and sent two friars to address them in front of a gathering crowd: "It is a great shame for us, servants of the Lord, that the bishop and the mayor hate each other in this way, without anyone bothering to pacify them." This was his message. Simple and short. Picture the scene. Look at the mystified faces of the onlookers (if only they'd had tabloid reporters at that time), the knowing nods, the cynical nudges, and the mayor and the bishop both feeling awkward and trying to retain a proper *bella figura* in public. You can't lose face in front of the public, they both knew. They were probably expecting a speech to be read from Francis. Or a scolding at least. Nothing like that. But there was something else coming.

Once again Francis did the unusual, the unexpected. He appealed to poetry. Yes, poetry. The poetry of pardon. He had composed a new verse for his now famous *Canticle of the Creatures* – also often referred to as *The Canticle of Brother Sun* – for this very encounter. Listen to this:

Praised be you, my Lord, for those who give
pardon for love of you
And bear infirmity and tribulation,
For by you, Most High, they will be
crowned.

There was a deep awkward silence on the Assisi
street when the messengers finished reading. People
stared blankly at the two friars and they stared back a bit
sheepishly, not knowing what to expect. Nervous coughs
broke the silence and the crowd of nobles and peasants
behind them began to shuffle uneasily. Heads began to
nod in apparent agreement. The bishop and the mayor,
scanning the faces of the crowd, knew this was a
challenge to their respective leadership roles. After brief
consultations with their advisers they became visibly
relaxed, and nodded their assent, their agreement.

They had come on board. The crowd drifted into
consenting nods and chatter and after a few moments
began to disperse. Soon the mayor and the bishop were
beaming as they stood side by side for "the media". Today
it would be a photo call for the tabloids. "Mayor and
Bishop Make Up", they would scream. The reconciliation
was no doubt the talk of the taverns that night. The rest,
as they keep telling us, is history.

In the context of those times, this verse, perhaps
divinely air-brushed, took away the hatred between the
mayor and bishop. From that day forward friendship and
respect was restored between them. Church and state
slept soundly that night. The mayor's wife, Rosaria, was
thrilled. She could once more hold her head high among
her society peers (even if some of them would continue to

secretly despise her and her contrived airs).

This was a dying forty-five-year-old Francis doing ministry; extreme ministry.

Chapter 25

Francis, Nature and Climate Change

The harmony between the Creator, humanity and creation as a whole was disrupted by our presuming to take the place of God and refusing to acknowledge our creaturely limitations. This in turn distorted our mandate to "have dominion" over the earth (cf. *Gen* 1: 28), to "till it and keep it" (*Gen* 2: 15). As a result, the originally harmonious relationship between human beings and nature became conflictual (cf. *Gen* 3: 17–19). It is significant that the harmony which Saint Francis of Assisi experienced with all creatures was seen as a healing of that rupture. Saint Bonaventure held that, through universal reconciliation with every creature, Saint Francis in some way returned to the state of original innocence.[40] This is a far cry from our situation today, where sin is manifest in all its destructive power in wars, the various forms of violence and abuse, the abandonment of the most vulnerable, and attacks on nature – *Pope Francis, Laudato Si No 66.*

Since we are talking about *The Canticle of the Creatures*, the "praise song" of all creation, composed by an ailing Francis, it is appropriate to recall once again that a grateful Blessed Pope John Paul II declared him Patron Saint of Ecologists and the Environment in 1980 (and consequently of all UN-sanctioned climate change conferences). This was because of Francis's prophetic engagement with all existence, his sensitivity to the delicate balances, links and relationships between water, light, fire, wind, plants, animals and humans. In his Canticle he was proposing an alternative view of nature, which raised eyebrows among Bible scholars, who leaned towards the idea that nature was to be used and controlled for the benefit of humanity. And look how crucially important that idea is today. Francis had already realised that "our world, our small blue planet in the midst of the vast Milky Way, is in truth a sacred sanctuary, a dwelling place for the divine".[9]

I am not really digressing when I report the following interconnections in the world of nature. Lawrence Anthony, author of *The Elephant Whisperer*, is a South African conservationist who speaks as one close to the life centre of nature. The plant and animal world, he writes, can confound us, especially in the realm of communications. Game rangers will tell you that rhino know about it the day before they are to be darted and relocated. They vanish into the woods and the camouflage shelter of the trees. In Asia it is well known that animals made for the safety of the hills before the

---

[9] These are the words of Mgr Dermot Lane of Dublin.

tsunami wave of 2004 hit the coastal areas. Animals, it seems, can hear without ears. And not just animals; plants can do it too. This is what Lawrence Anthony tells us:

> The acacia tree not only understands it's under attack when browsed by antelope or giraffe, it quickly injects tannin into its leaves making them taste bitter. The tree then releases a scent, a pheromone, into the air to warn other acacias in the area of the potential danger. These neighbouring trees receive the warning and immediately start producing tannin themselves in anticipation of an attack. *The Elephant Whisperer*, p. 49.

Without a brain, this author asks, how can a tree know it has a family and neighbour to protect? What is the life force, the vital ingredient of existence that is driving the secret world of nature? Did Francis know something about the hidden life of nature, secrets of creation that we don't know, even in the twenty-first century? Did he have a sixth sense that made him a nature or animal "whisperer"? Think of the wolf of Gubbio; think of the birds.

Francis was not an ecologist but he had the sensitivity and discernment of one. He was not a conservationist but he had the soul and passion of one. Francis was not a poet but he produced a poem in praise of creation – human, animal and plant life – that still echoes globally after eight hundred years. Did the vast human and natural vistas of North Africa induce new wonder in the expanding mind of the Poverello? The wonder of his African experience may well have led him to question not only his narrow provincial values but also to reimagine the sheer vastness and immensity of creation. (As Nobel prize-winning novelist Doris Lessing, who grew up in Africa, said, "Africa gives you the knowledge that man is a small creature among other creatures in a large landscape"). It was with this vision of Africa still fresh in mind that Francis composed *The Canticle of the Creatures*. Pope Francis concurs: "Everything is related, and we human beings are united as brothers and sisters on a wonderful pilgrimage, woven together by the love God has for each of his creatures and which also unites us in fond affection with brother sun, sister moon, brother river and mother earth" (*Pope Francis, Laudato Si no 92*).

But what makes Francis different from ecologists, conservationists, and even poets, is that he unashamedly attributes it all to God's glory – amazingly mirrored, living and dwelling across the seas and landscapes of planet earth and the great far beyond.

At Sister Clare's convent, when he knew he was dying, Francis wrote his *Canticle of the Creatures*, a beautiful poem opening up in praise of all created things. Francis was increasingly seeing the bigger picture. Was the world not his church; was the cosmos not his cathedral?

Another first for the saint of Assisi. And Pope Francis agrees.

Chapter 26

"I'm Spiritual but not Religious" He Said

Pope Francis wants you to know that we're all Franciscans now – *John L Allen, Jr, senior correspondent for the National Catholic Reporter and Senior Vatican analyst for CNN*

Francis's often unorthodox and original solutions to problems may have appeared flamboyant at times, but they were simply inspirations from a soul close to God. His increasing creative interventions in society touched many by their sheer proactive inventiveness. "Nobody showed me what to do but the Most High revealed to me that I had to live according to the Holy Gospel", he always said to surprised listeners. Sr Rose Fernando, FMM teaches:

> Experience shows that preference needs to be given to early intervention. As one woman from Kosovo said at the Hague Conference, 'Peace workers need to be at the right place at the right time before violence escalates. Otherwise we are just counting our mistakes.' (International Franciscan Congress: *Instruments of Peace Led by the Spirit, Vossenack, Germany, 2000, p. 43*).

Not all the brothers were convinced about Francis

being constantly on the move in the name of peace building. Some Franciscan dissenters, especially the more housebound, complained about his constant peace initiatives in faraway places. He was needed at home, they grumbled. But Francis ignored them; prompted and assured by God. Remember he had been through the mill, had seen the violence, had felt the pain and was in no mood to submit to spiritual blackmail or immature pettiness. Looking back, we now can see that Francis was evolving into a new spirituality within the formalised religion of the Church. A new spirituality within the community of the faithful.

> "Up to this point, most of Christian spirituality was based in desert asceticism, monastic discipline, theories of prayer, or academic theology ... but not in a kind of practical Christianity that could be lived in the streets of the world. Many rightly say Francis emphasised an imitation and love of the humanity of Jesus, not just the worshipping of his divinity" (*Richard Rohr's Daily Meditations, Thursday August 27, 2015*).

Francis distinguishes himself in being both religious and spiritual. The sex abuse scandal in the church recently proves the point. We keep coming back to it. Because of the clerical scandals of his time, many thousands had left the Church in protest. They formed new sects. Assisi itself was a stronghold of the Albigensians, but Francis wasn't tempted by them. Today, northern hemisphere people leave the Church because of similar scandals, but they don't form new sects. They "secularise", they somehow develop or catch blowing in the wind their own set of beliefs to get them through their immediate circumstances. The secular is the new religion. Times have changed.

Francis had this option – to leave or to stay. But his spirituality, his personal closeness to Christ, drew him back from the brink. He knew, somehow, that he had to take responsibility for the shortcomings of the Church, of the wounded Body of Christ. His deeply grounded spirituality would not let him desert the community of the people of God. For him, to turn his back on this community, the Church, would have been a refusal to face human brokenness, a refusal to accept human frailty, and a refusal to shoulder the Cross as part of our earthly journey. He knew he could not walk away from the more than a thousand years of tested spirituality that had produced great saints, martyrs, cultures, religions and civilisations. Interestingly, Francis's realisation that church and spirituality are one, can be a kind of response – a sort of eight-hundred-year-old caution – to those good people today who assert proudly in media interviews: "I'm spiritual, but I'm not religious."

Can one really be spiritual and ignore centuries of religious reflection and spirituality?

Chapter 27

Francis, Mary and Marian Ministry

We have relegated the saints to a pink and blue and gold world of plaster statuary that belongs to the past; it is a hangover, a relic, of the Dark Ages ... We are content to place a statue of Francis of Assisi in the middle of a bird bath and let the whole business of the saints go to that – *Chauncie Kilmer Myers*

Mary was special for Francis. His love for the Blessed Mother of God was "inexpressible". "Towards the Mother of Jesus he was filled with an inexpressible love because it was she who made the Lord of majesty our brother," his biographer, Thomas of Celano, reports. Francis lived close to the mind of Mary. He began to see himself as her peacemaker and her messenger of reconciliation. This was not unusual. It was not strange. It was part of his unfolding journey. Part of his new self.

Significantly, in almost all the visions of Our Lady in modern times, Mary begs her children to engage the world in fasting, prayer, peace-building and reconciliation. This is very much a Marian message. It is surely a direct invitation, an appeal from Our Lady to Marian pilgrims and devotees to become prayerful activists in justice-making and peace-building in their parishes and around the world. After all the litanies say

Mary is our "Mirror of Justice". This is the language of Pope Francis. It is also the language of Lourdes, Medjugorje and Knock. It is only now that the apparitions at Medjugorje and Kibeho are being seen in the context of the bloody wars in Bosnia and Rwanda that followed the apparitions.

Francis would never have known the magnificent Pastoral Letter of the South African Bishops in 1988 on the Woman of Nazareth which projects an earthly biblical image of Mary rather different from that of the heavenly appearances at Lourdes, Knock, Fatima, Medjugorje or Kibeho (Rwanda); the Mary of the Bible, as distinct from the Mary of the visions.

The intimate life of the pregnant seventeen year old Mary; her courageous *fiat*; the lonely fears she felt after the angel Gabriel left; the unpredictable shocks when she visited her aunt, Elizabeth; more visions and more guidance from new dreams; Joseph and *his* life-changing dreams; the cave birth (Joseph was a carpenter not a midwife or a male nurse); strange groups of visitors, the shepherds and so-called kings or astrologers from foreign places they had never heard of; Herod, a serial killer, bent on killing the child Jesus leading to the eventual hurried departure of the Holy Family for the safety of Africa. These are the immediate circumstances leading to the coming of God to our world. No hotels, ceremonial guards, car cavalcades with flashing lights, no build-up of media hype for of the coming event, no receptions and speeches ... The toll on the family who had simply come to register themselves must have been terrible. Christians around the world "celebrate" these events during the Christmas period even if the Holy

Family itself saw little to celebrate!

And then there is the litany of the many praises of Our Lady. Like Muslims fingering on their beads the many names of Allah. When I was young my mother intoned the litany to Our Lady every evening immediately after the family rosary. She knew these exotic names for Mary off by heart. It was her firm Northern Ireland faith. We younger ones knew that if for any reason she could not be present, the rosary led by my father would be short and sweet that evening. Because he didn't know the litanies like my Ma. It meant more time for play with pals on the streets outside. None of us understood much of the eloquent language, the beautiful sophisticated names attributed to Mary in the litanies: Spiritual Vessel, Mystical Rose, Tower of David, House of Gold, Gate of Heaven, Ark of the Covenant, Queen of Virgins ... We were culture Catholics, creatures of our time, we didn't ask. They were above and beyond us. St Francis also would not have understood them. But they were impressive on the ear and taught us that Mary was worthy of praise, any type of praise. All very biblical of course, and much from the gospel of Luke.

Decades later living far away from my foundations I had to rethink my position, reappraise my understanding about the litanies of Mary. The local situation called for a Lady familiar with the poor on the streets. In Africa many chiefs have praise singers who go before them singing the praises of their lives and achievements on ceremonial occasions. Could I attempt to do the same for Mary? I tried to come up with something that I think Francis would have been proud of. I dared to suggest that the forty-nine distinct modes of

Mary (the litany) could be enriched with new and equally authentic Christian reflections. Some examples: Mary, (in Bethlehem) Mother of the homeless. Mary (in Africa) Mother of exiles; Mary (in Jerusalem) mother of Small Christian Communities, Mother of the Oppressed, Model of Tolerance, Model of Risk, Model of Hope, of Marginalised Women, Political Refugee, Mother of the Non-Violent, Mary, fearless Mother, Queen of our Ancestors, Pray for us ...

To say nothing of Mary's social and political observations in her mighty Magnificat savoured by many in the developing world.

Of course Francis's praises of Mary are very much a litany in themselves:

Hail, O Lady, holy Queen,
Mary, holy Mother of God;
You are the virgin made *church* ...
Hail, His Palace!
Hail, His Tabernacle!
Hail, His Home!
Hail, His Robe!
Hail, His Servant!
Hail, His Mother ...

He would, however, be comfortable when we remember Mary of Bethlehem. The whole purpose of his sacred Christmas "pantomime" at Greccio was to bring us back to our roots and as close as possible to the Bethlehem event.

Mary of the Poor and Disadvantaged loved by

Francis, Pray for us.

Mary the most powerful woman in the world (*National Geographic, December 2015*), Pray for us.

Chapter 28

The Jovial Death of Francis

Brother Doctor, do not be afraid of telling me the closeness of death. It is for me the door to life – *St Francis, shortly before his death in 1226*

By now Francis was a badly preserved forty-something. His Mediterranean campaign was over. The travels, the shipwreck, the disappointments and the wars had taken their toll. He was back in Assisi where it all began. The brothers sensed the end was near. What procedure do you follow when a living saint, your founder, is dying?

Francis's death was as extraordinary as his life had been. Brother Elias, General of the Order chastised Francis, on his deathbed:

> Father, I am very glad that you feel so much joy; but I fear that in the city, where they take you for a saint, it would be scandalous for them to see that you are not preparing properly for a good death.

"Do not be troubled," Francis answered him, "with all my sufferings I feel so close to God that I can do nothing but sing." Just before he died, Francis asked his brothers to carry him to the spot where they had first lived together, at St Mary of the Angels. There were a few other brothers and friends there too when he made the request. They wondered, even though they revered him powerfully, what he was up to now that he was on the threshold of death. But they had learned over time to be very cautious about challenging his many divine inspirations. They had grown to expect the unpredictable Holy Spirit to guide his ways: they did what he asked. As he lay dying, Francis again asked the brothers to sing God's praises. That was a very alive gesture from a half-blind dying man with the wasted body of a concentration camp inmate. A very unashamedly faith-filled gesture. An unmistakable desire to be with the Lord as soon as possible. He was bridging the chasm between this world and Heaven. He wrote a note blessing his friend Clare and her sisters, and absolved the brothers and sisters – together – for any failures in following his previous counsels in their new religious life. He even called Lady Jacoba to his bedside, waiving the rule that forbade women from entering the enclosure. There was nothing conventional about Francis. Then he astonished them even further. In a Last Supper-like gesture, and straining for strength, he shared bread with all present. Totally Christ-like. It was an unforgettable moment of communion and community. Later he murmurs, almost inaudibly, that he wants to be laid naked on the earth as a final salute and acknowledgement of Christ, naked and crucified, on the lonely hill of Calvary. To confirm his closeness to all things earthly, his fraternal identification, he insists that the brothers sprinkle him with ashes – for he was soon to become dust and ashes.

It was as if these actions, these gestures, strange to the uninitiated, were premeditated, pre-planned. It was as if he had a special familiarity, even before death, with the here and the hereafter. As if he had a foot in both, even while he lived. Francis was offering the world a new look at death, a new way of dying. No other saint has done this. No other saint has given this type of example. And all this after showing the world a completely new way of living according to the Gospel of our Lord Jesus Christ.

The phenomenon of Francis's close friendship with death was at least partly due to his tender relationship with all the elements and creatures of our earth, as illustrated in his *Canticle of the Creatures*. This so often is the experience of the poor and indigenous peoples of the world. In making this point Br Bienvenido Baisas, OFM, of Sri Lanka pointedly adds that "people who have been alienated from creation by the superficial airs of technological life cannot but be hostile to death".

His liturgy of passing and parting continues.

He asked to be brought outside one more time. He blessed his turbulent home town, Assisi, gleaming and nestling in the evening sun against a backdrop of Umbrian hills. This was poignant because the town had some unhappy memories for him. Memories difficult to erase and forget. God had revealed to him his "wrongness of judgement" on Assisi so his blessing was a gesture of love, mercy and reconciliation. Indoors again, surrounded by brothers and friends, Francis breathed his final, timeless, "Welcome, Sister Death", gently slumped sideways, and was gone.

So at his last great public liturgy, Francis of Assisi was master of ceremonies, and chief celebrant. Organised and driven by his indomitable spirit, his unorthodox liturgies – the crib at Greccio and his holy death – are still celebrated throughout the world eight hundred years later.

His liturgies were for damaged people. For and with the poor.

Reconciled with death, and courteous as always, at the young age of forty-four he welcomed "Sister Death", and died singing the final verse of his *Canticle of the Creatures*:

> Be praised, my Lord, through our sister Bodily Death,
> from whose embrace no living person can escape.
> Woe to those who die in mortal sin!
> Happy those she finds doing Your most holy will.
> The second death can do no harm to them.

A question: It would be impossible today to live like a medieval Francis. But perhaps we can live like a modern St Francis? For eight hundred years, millions of his followers, including Pope Francis, have tried to do just that – and, in small ways, they have succeeded.

AFTER WORD

Now that you've read the story are you upset, glad or left thoughtful?

- How do you feel about this Francis of history?
- Are lovers of St Francis serious about Francis as the patron saint of ecologists and the unity of the cosmos?
- Are there two versions of St Francis? The reverent church-bound sacramental saint who loved animals and the itinerant backpacker, preacher of peace, love and reconciliation?
- Why do you think Francis "invented" his own liturgy to suit an occasion?
- Francis often found himself reading the signs of the times at short notice. This led him to make urgent social interventions in his society. What shape might similar social interventions take today?
- How would St Francis fit into religious life today?